Ghosts of Hollywood III

Marla Brooks

Schiffer Publishing Ltd

4880 Lower Valley Road, Atglen, Pennsylvania 19310

Other Schiffer Books by Marla Brooks:

Workplace Spells, 978-0-7643-3136-7, $19.99
Hollywood Ghosts: The Show Still Goes On, 978-0-7643-2883-1, $14.95
Hollywood Ghosts II: Talking to Spirits, 978-0-7643-2997-5, $14.99

Schiffer Books are available at special discounts for bulk purchases for sales promotions or premiums. Special editions, including personalized covers, corporate imprints, and excerpts can be created in large quantities for special needs. For more information contact the publisher:

Schiffer Publishing Ltd.
4880 Lower Valley Road
Atglen, PA 19310
Phone: (610) 593-1777; Fax: (610) 593-2002
E-mail: Info@schifferbooks.com

For the largest selection of fine reference books on this and related subjects, please visit our web site at **www.schifferbooks.com**
We are always looking for people to write books on new and related subjects. If you have an idea for a book please contact us at the above address.

This book may be purchased from the publisher. Include $5.00 for shipping.
Please try your bookstore first. You may write for a free catalog.

In Europe, Schiffer books are distributed by
Bushwood Books
6 Marksbury Ave.
Kew Gardens
Surrey TW9 4JF England
Phone: 44 (0) 20 8392-8585; Fax: 44 (0) 20 8392-9876
E-mail: info@bushwoodbooks.co.uk
Website: www.bushwoodbooks.co.uk
Free postage in the U.K., Europe; air mail at cost.

Copyright © 2009 by Marla Brooks
Library of Congress Control Number: 2008939072

Designed by Stephanie Daugherty
Type set in Rosemary Roman/New Baskerville BT

ISBN: 978-0-7643-3201-2
Printed in the United States of America

Dedication

To friends and loved ones on the other side who are always around to remind us that there is still more to come.

Acknowledgements

A gain I must give credit where credit is due, because without friends like psychic Victoria Gross, paranormal investigator and videographer Barry Conrad, and Hollywood historian Scott Michaels, who are always up for a new investigation despite their busy schedules, I'd be totally lost. Then there's Dinah Roseberry at Schiffer Books who not only makes sure it all gets done right, but has also become a very good friend in the process. And to Kenny Kingston, Michael J. Kouri, and Mark Nelson, I thank them for sharing their time, their wisdom, and generosity of spirit with me.

A very special nod goes to David Wells, who once again, and despite facing his own pressing deadlines and work commitments, managed to make some time for me as well, and David, I can't thank you enough.

And finally, to Ken Grogg, thank you for all your love and support throughout this book after book after book odyssey of mine. I know it must have seemed like I was in a world of my own, but I really had the best of both worlds.

Bright blessings on you all.

Foreword by David Wells

We all have dreams, hopes, wishes and ambitions and with a lot of energy, we are told they can come true, regardless of the obstacles put in front of us. Whilst subscribing to that theory, I also recognize that some dreams are harder to get to than others and the energy required may be too much, or could it be we actually prefer something else and on a subconscious level we settle?

If you have settled, then suddenly find yourself without the baggage of a physical body or the limitations of time and space, would you do things differently? Free will is ours to do with as we please, for some, the astral worlds and free will means time to download what we have learned in our incarnation; for others, it seems pursuing some unfinished business is high on our heavenly 'to do' list.

Hollywood holds court and welcomes wannabes with have-used-to-be, shining stars that refuse to dim their lights and disgruntled players who never had the chance to shine; all full of energy directed by free will and aimed at making their point—now they write the scripts.

Hauntings come in many ways, shapes, and forms, as do we. Some spirits want to attract attention to dance and be appreciated, some to complain you never gave them a chance, and some to simply tell their story to anyone who will or indeed can, listen.

In a culture obsessed with celebrity, it's hardly surprising we cannot leave them alone, even when they are dead. But the truth is, if they chose to move away, they could—some spirits seem to want the attention for eternity. Macabre or fascinating? It's about interaction, a performance with an audience; one without the other doesn't work.

Marla explores the stage behind the stage, the screen behind the screen, and the life behind this life—what better place than Hollywood where all you have to do is shine a light and there they are...

—David Wells
Psychic Medium

Table of Contents

Contents

Introduction

With the advent of the Hollywood film industry at the turn of the twentieth century, our fair city evolved from a quiet little hamlet out in the middle of nowhere into the film capital of the world.

Since that time, men, women, and children from all over the country have flocked to Hollywood to try and make a name for themselves on the silver screen. But in the early days of silent movies the actors and actresses appearing in these films were not publicized as they are now and did as much work behind the scenes as in front of the camera. Some of the performers had to help build the sets, do clean up, and other chores around the film studio. As the movie-going public became more interested in the performers who attracted their attention, however, the curiosity to know more about them made the movie studios and producers rethink their policy. And as the demand increased, sometime around 1912, the studios began publicizing the names of their leading women and men.

While the film industry has only been around for a hundred years or so, the acting profession goes back more than 2,000 years. The first recorded case of an actor's performance took place in 534 BC when the Greek poet Thespis stepped on to the stage at the *Theatre Dionysus* and became the first known person to speak words as a character in a play or story. Prior to Thespis, stories were only known to be told in song and dance and in third person narrative. In honor of Thespis, actors are now commonly called *Thespians*. Theatrical legend to this day maintains that Thespis exists as a mischievous spirit,

and disasters in the theatre are sometimes blamed on his ghostly intervention.

In recent times actors have been held in the highest regard but that wasn't always so. Traditionally, they were not people of high status, and in the Early Middle Ages, traveling acting troupes were often viewed with distrust. In many parts of Europe, actors could not even receive a Christian burial, and traditional beliefs of the region and time period held that this left any actor forever condemned.

In the beginning, it was only men could become actors. In ancient Greece and Rome and in the medieval world, it was considered disgraceful for a woman to go up on stage, and this belief continued right up until the seventeenth century. In Japan, men took over the female roles in kabuki theatre when women were banned from performing during the Edo period.

In the time of William Shakespeare, women's roles were generally played by men or boys. The British prohibition was ended in the reign of Charles II who rather enjoyed watching female actors.

In today's Hollywood, no such taboos exist. In fact, the word *taboo* doesn't seem to exist either, except when it comes to the subject of death. It's one thing to "die on stage," meaning you've given a really bad performance, but if that happens, there's usually the chance for the actor to redeem him/herself at a later date. But dying, as in "ceasing to exist" is, if you'll excuse the pun, a fate worse than death because there is no chance of redemption or, in some cases, the fear of being forgotten.

It's my belief that many Hollywood ghosts come back just because they miss the limelight and want to keep their

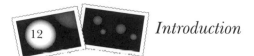

names alive. I'm sure the same could be said for other famous folk like William Shakespeare, Rembrandt, or King Henry VIII. They have all left a legacy that they may feel needs looking after. But in Hollywood, where "ego" is everyone's middle name, the return rate of celebrity spirits seems to be much higher.

People often ask me if I think Hollywood has more ghosts than anywhere else and my stock answer is, "Probably not, but our ghosts are definitely more famous."

Having said that, I've lately begun to wonder if I'm selling Hollywood short in the ghost census. After all, this is my third book on Hollywood ghosts and I'm not anywhere near running out of places to investigate and stories to be told. New information comes to light every day and frankly, it's hard to keep up.

I get many of my leads when I'm not even looking or them. Like the day I went to Leeza Gibbons' office to tape a couple of segments for her radio show *Hollywood Confidential*. There I met a man named Tom Gregory who said he owned Gary Cooper's old house and thought it might be haunted. That comment lead to a wonderful investigation of the actor's former home and he turned out to be the perfect host!

Then there was the day that I dragged my psychic friend Victoria Gross over to the LaBrea Tar Pits thinking that someone might have inadvertently lost their life many years ago by falling into the sticky goo and wanted to come back and tell us all about their tragic demise.

After we walked around the pits for several minutes inhaling much more stinky methane gas than was tolerable, Victoria concluded that the area was spirit free, but when

we strolled into the Page Museum gift shop just a few yards away, we met an "ethereal" shopper.

With a population of about 300,000 living residents, one has to wonder whether or not there are more ghosts than human beings in this town, especially when you consider the vast number of folks who have lived and died in Hollywood over the past century. It seems as though no matter where you go or who you talk to in Hollywood, there is either a ghost or ghost story around every corner.

Gary Cooper's House

When I was at Leeza Gibbons' office taping a couple of segments for her radio show *Hollywood Confidential*, I was introduced to Tom Gregory. Tom appears regularly on Leeza's show.

Victoria Gross was with me that day and Tom mentioned that he owned the house that Gary Cooper had lived (and died) in. He also said he thought the house might be haunted. Tom, a non-smoker, said that he had smelled cigarette smoke inside the house on several occasions, (Cooper was a heavy smoker) and mentioned that there were a few other odd things about the house that lead him to the conclusion that perhaps Gary Cooper might still be around.

This was an intriguing revelation so I asked Tom if it would be possible for us to come out to the house sometime and do an investigation and he said yes.

To millions of his fans, Gary Cooper represented the *All-American Man*. The tall, handsome actor with the steely blue eyes made over one hundred films and was renowned for his quiet, understated acting style.

Although he was known as a man of very few words, Cooper was once quoted as saying, "All this business about me never saying anything is a piece of crap."

An enduring joke about the actor's taciturn speech habits all started with a 1938 appearance on the popular Edgar Bergen and Charlie McCarthy radio program. The show had Cooper being asked every type of question and giving only "Yup" as a response until asked if he couldn't say anything but "Yup." He answered with a succinct

Poolside view of Gary Cooper' house.

"Nope." The *yup-nope* business would grow into a legend, and the actor would often resort to it for comic effect in everyday conversation. It remains associated with him even today.

Cooper received five Oscar nominations for Best Actor, winning twice. He also received an Honorary Award from the Motion Picture Academy in 1961 just shortly before his death. At the time, it was reported that he couldn't attend the ceremony because of a pinched nerve in his back and his friend Jimmy Stewart accepted the accolade for him. This wasn't the first Oscar ceremony Cooper missed. Back in 1953, and bedridden with an ulcer, he wasn't able to pick up his coveted statuette in the Best Actor category for the film *High Noon* which to some is considered his finest role. Instead, he asked John Wayne to accept it on his behalf which is a bit ironic because of Wayne's stated distaste for the film.

Jimmy Stewart's emotional speech that Oscar night in 1961 hinted that something was seriously wrong, and the next day newspapers all over the world ran the headline, "Gary Cooper has cancer."

That previous spring, the actor underwent two operations, one for prostate cancer, and then a short while later, a part of his colon was removed which was found to be cancerous as well. After the second operation, the doctors were sure that Cooper was cancer-free and he recovered sufficiently to travel to England and star in the movie *The Naked Edge* (which was released posthumously), but during production, he complained of pain in his neck and shoulders. When he returned home and went back to the doctor, the actor learned that the cancer had metastasized to his lungs and bones. He took the diagnosis in stride and opted not to take aggressive measures as far as treatment was concerned and said, "If it is God's will, that's all right too."

Once the word was out that Cooper was indeed on his death bed, messages poured in from friends, well-wishers, and dignitaries from all over the world, including Pope John XXIII, former Vice President Richard Nixon, Pablo Picasso, Queen Elizabeth II of England, Princess Grace (Grace Kelly) of Monaco, John Wayne, Ernest Hemingway, former President Dwight D. Eisenhower, Bob Hope, and Jack Benny. The newly inaugurated President John F. Kennedy called from Washington and couldn't get through on Cooper's busy phone, but kept trying and finally got through on the second day—he spoke with Cooper for seven minutes.

The actor quietly passed away at the age of sixty on May 13, 1961, just a month after the news of his

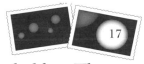

illness had been revealed. His funeral was held at The Church of the Good Shepherd in Beverly Hills. One of the eulogies delivered made reference to the acting profession: "Death is like the theater. You enter and it is dark. Then the curtain rises and before you is a bright, new, wonderful light."

Cooper's pallbearers included close friends James Stewart, Henry Hathaway, Jack Benny, William Goetz, Jerry Wald, and Charles Feldman. His wife, Rocky, and daughter, Maria, walked behind the casket, alongside Cooper's eighty-seven-year-old mother, Alice, and his brother, Arthur, as it was borne through the church to the hearse out on Santa Monica Boulevard. Among the top names of Hollywood attending the services were Dean Martin, Marlene Dietrich, Randolph Scott, Burt Lancaster, Jimmy Durante, John Wayne, George Burns and Gracie Allen, Fred Astaire, Bob Hope, Dinah Shore, and Frank Sinatra. In an interesting side note, Frank Sinatra's funeral was held at the same church thirty-seven years later, almost to the day.

Gary Cooper was loved for his wholesome on-screen persona, but in his private life, he was known as a lover. Cooper had high-profile relationships with actresses Clara Bow, Lupe Vélez, the American-born socialite-spy Countess Carla Dentice di Frasso, and with several famous co-stars, including Marlene Dietrich, Grace Kelly, and Patricia Neal.

Ms. Bow was something of a legend in her own time. She was the epitome of the uninhibited free-spirited flapper both in her films and in her private life. She and Cooper entered into a torrid affair, and Clara insisted on his being cast in her latest movie, *It*. Even though his role was only a two-scene bit, publicity about their affair took hold, with the press proclaiming that the "It" Girl had found her "It" Boy.

When the handsome actor moved in with Mexican Spitfire Lupe Velez a few years later, their union caused quite a stir, because at the time, an unmarried couple living together was pretty much unheard of. And beyond that, Cooper's mother had an intense dislike for Lupe.

"I'm not good enough for him, I know that," Velez said shortly after their breakup, "but I tried to make him happy. I did make him happy. I would have done anything in the world for him. His mother—I hope she never cries the tears that I have cried. I hope she never knows the suffering I have known. I don't hate her, that much. She said I wasn't good enough for Gary. She told him that when I was in New York, I was seeing other men. She told him that I wasn't faithful to him. He believed what she told him."

Their brawls were notorious and the relationship finally ended when Gary was boarding the Twentieth Century train to Chicago one fateful day after Velez learned that Cooper had no intention of marrying her. Vengeful Lupe arrived at the station, pulled a gun and shot several times at her lover, narrowly missing his head. Cooper dove into the car and Velez quickly stormed out of the station, swearing at her lack of marksmanship.

In 1933, Cooper went on to marry Veronica (Rocky) Balfe, a New York Roman Catholic socialite who had briefly acted under the name of Sandra Shaw. She appeared in the film *No Other Woman*, but her most widely-seen role was in *King Kong*, as the woman dropped by Kong. Her third and final movie was *Blood Money*.

Veronica's father was governor of the New York Stock Exchange, and during the 1930s she became the California state women's Skeet Champion. She and Cooper had one child, Maria. The Coopers separated between 1951 and 1954, supposedly because of his reported affairs with his leading ladies.

Cooper met actress Marlene Dietrich during filming of *Morocco* in 1930 and the affair carried on for several years. Rocky served Dietrich with a writ during divorce proceedings but the writ, and the divorce action, was dropped.

A few years later, Cooper and Patricia Neal began a torrid affair. They appeared in three films together in 1949-50, including *The Fountainhead*. That affair led to Cooper's separation from his wife.

"Gary Cooper was in love with Patricia Neal for many years," said Tom Gregory, "and when they broke up, he moved into this house with his wife. This was their 'get back together' home."

The Coopers enjoyed a great life in their ultra-modern home in Holmby Hills which was built in the early 1950s. Designed by architect Quincy Jones (with a little bit of input from Cooper), the house was full of push-button gadgets and special accommodations for a man of Cooper's height.

The actor's last days were spent quietly in the house, and six days after his sixtieth birthday, Gary Cooper lapsed into a coma and died the following afternoon.

Three days before we were set to go do the investigation of Gary Cooper's house, I was scheduled to do a radio show promoting my first book, *Ghosts of Hollywood: The Show Still Goes On*. Psychic Lisa J. Smith was going to co-host

the show and she got in touch with me a couple of hours before airtime to say hello.

During the course of our phone conversation, I mentioned that we were going to be doing the investigation at the Cooper house and kind of joked that I was hoping that Gary Cooper would be there to greet us. Much to my surprise, Lisa said that Mr. Cooper was eavesdropping on our conversation and told her to let me know that he would indeed be at the house when we got there and seemed to be glad we were coming. With that in mind, I couldn't wait to begin our investigation.

We were two team members short on the day of the investigation. It was just Victoria Gross and I who were privileged to visit the magnificent home. As we drove though the front gates and up the winding road towards the house, it felt as though we'd entered a time warp. There was a definite "Old Hollywood" feel about the property and its park-like setting.

Tom Gregory met us as we parked the car and walked us in through the front door. No art director could have captured the feel of Hollywood's Golden Era better than the current owners who have done a magnificent job of retaining the feel and integrity of the home as it was when Cooper was in residence.

As we walked into the home's huge kitchen, I couldn't help but remember something I'd read in passing about Gary Cooper's prodigious appetite. The article said that during his early years in Hollywood, working odd jobs and living with his parents, he said with some comic exaggeration, that his "starvation diet" at the time ran to no less than a dozen eggs a day, a couple of loaves of bread, a platter of bacon,

The living room at the Cooper house with quite a few orbs.

and just enough pork chops between meals to keep him going until he got home for supper, and that his specialty on hunting trips was gargantuan: wild duck covered with bacon strips, enhanced by four eggs and steak. He could eat a cherry pie and drink a quart of milk for lunch. And yet, no matter how much he ate, he always remained thin.

While we were unpacking our gear and getting ready for Tom to show us around, I couldn't help feeling as though we were intruding, somehow; not on Tom, exactly, but on Gary Cooper. After all, this was his private space away from the limelight, his beloved home and, on an even more personal level, this was the place where he died… in a bedroom just down the hall.

It seemed appropriate to make that bedroom the first stop on our tour of the home, and while I didn't get

Victoria Gross in the bedroom where Gary Cooper died.

the impression that we weren't supposed to be there, I just couldn't shake the feeling that we were disturbing the sanctity of Gary Cooper's transition between life and death and let Tom and Victoria enter the room before me.

The bedroom furniture has been rearranged since Cooper's passing, and the spot where the actor lay on his deathbed is now taken up by a small credenza of sorts. I walked over to the spot where the actor breathed his last and although it was rather eerie to know that someone had died right there, the area seemed rather benign to me and I didn't get the impression that Cooper's spirit was even around.

Victoria didn't seem to think that the actor was around, either, but she did pick up the energy of a

**This is the spot where Gary Cooper passed away.
The bed now sits on the other side of the room.**

woman who she described as a tall blond with shoulder-length hair. She got the impression that this was someone who frequented the house, not just a guest who might have come to a party. "Her energy is so strong. I get the feeling that she might have been a caretaker of some sort."

While Tom, who is quite knowledgeable about Cooper's life in the house and the others who spent time there as well, didn't recognize who that woman spirit might be, he had a few thoughts about the room itself.

"This is a room that's always felt uneasy to me," he told us. "It's as if it never settled. The room itself has never found a home with us. It's been two different offices and a bedroom, but none of them ever really worked. I was actually thinking about converting the room into a closet because it just isn't working. And right in front of that shower," he said, pointing to the adjacent bathroom, "there is an odd feeling to me and a sense of movement between the bathroom and his bedroom. And when you get out of the shower and are toweling off, you always get the sense that you're being watched."

And to prove his point about the odd-feeling bathroom, Tom added, "I own one of only six known signed photos of Abraham Lincoln and I had the photo hanging in the bathroom and I really noticed a big difference in the amount of energy it brought in. Ultimately I wound up putting it away," he admitted. "I paid over one hundred grand for the picture and now it's in a drawer because it was just too weird. It's weird when you get something that you know someone with so much weight to who they were touched it."

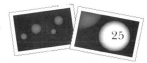

My mood was a bit somber when we walked into the bedroom because this was a place of death, but Victoria commented that she thought that the energy in the room was very light-hearted for the most part. She also, though, felt a bit of confusion, and thought she might be picking up on some residual energy left over from right before the actor passed away. She felt as though he was trying to talk, but was having a great deal of difficulty being understood.

"I feel like at the end, there was a real battle going on within him and nobody quite understood what he was saying. Like some kind of unfinished business. There was a conflict right at the end, and I'd say it had something to do with a will, and did he have a daughter?" she asked. "I'm picking up a daughter who may have been part of the conflict. He loved his daughter but I'm sensing some kind of triangle thing going on and it had to do with the last days of his life and something about a will. There's a man in the peripheral that was trying to infiltrate in regards to the will."

With all that talk about a will, I couldn't help being reminded of the poignant scene in *High Noon* when Cooper's character sat down to make out his last will and testament just before a man who he put behind bars is due to arrive on the high noon train to seek his revenge.

A few minutes later, we left the bedroom and continued down the long hall and into a room at the far end that looked like it was being used as an office. Victoria said she felt as though there was someone on the other side of the glass doors looking in at us and she felt as though it was a woman's spirit.

Victoria saw a woman spirit looking at us from behind these glass doors.

"This isn't the woman I felt in Cooper's bedroom," she said. "This one is not from days gone by. She's more recent than that. I see her as an elderly woman and she's kind of a watchful soul, just peering in from the outside as if to keep an eye on us."

Victoria's acknowledging the old woman outside seemed to open a floodgate and soon we were joined by several others. "They're starting to come in now," she said. "They weren't here when we first came in but they're here now."

"There's a big guy, fat, big belly who has a cigar in his mouth that just came in and I think the turmoil people feel in this house is related to him, as is the elderly woman I just mentioned. I see her as a crouching figure, and I get the feeling that she was very much controlled. I think she might be this guy's wife."

When we walked into the next bedroom, Victoria felt a very strong presence and described a little boy spirit also outside looking in, about five to seven years old with brownish-black hair. "I'm fairly certain that this was not the strong spirit energy I immediately felt as we walked into this room, but he's here as well."

I also felt a strong presence in that room as well, and it really made me feel uncomfortable. In fact, it felt as though I was being "cloaked" by a spirit who seemed to be hovering right behind me. It was definitely a male energy; he was a very strong presence and I got the impression that he didn't want us there. I didn't feel threatened, exactly, but I definitely got the message that he wanted us out of there, as if this was his private space and that we were intruding. Victoria was feeling uneasy as well, and it appeared that the man had no intention of trying to

The "ghoulish" bedroom that wanted us out!

communicate with us other than using scare tactics, so we decided to move on.

Earlier during our investigation, Tom had mentioned that a man with possible mob connections bought the house after Gary Cooper died, and on our way out of the room, I couldn't help but wonder if this was they spirit we had just encountered.

Tom didn't know the man's name but I was able to do a subsequent title search the next day and found out who purchased the Cooper estate after the actor's death. His name was Beldon R. Katelmann. My research did not tie Mr. Katleman to any sort of mob activity, but he *was* a very powerful man.

Beldon Katleman was a casino owner who is widely credited with the first Las Vegas all-you-can-eat buffet. From the late 1940s, until it was destroyed by a fire in 1960, he owned and operated El Rancho Vegas, Las Vegas' first resort hotel and casino. In an effort to keep patrons in his casino, Katleman came up with the idea of the $1 Midnight Chuck Wagon Buffet in 1947.

Katleman inherited the hotel from his uncle, Maurice Katleman. It's said that Beldon was a vigorous and determined man who reveled in running his own enterprises. He guided El Rancho through its heyday, and the resort became famous for its "big name" entertainment. Stars who appeared at the resort included Pearl Bailey, Milton Berle, Lena Horne, Sophie Tucker, Rudy Vallee, and famous stripper Lili St. Cyr. The resort hosted the weddings of Steve Lawrence and Eydie Gorme, Paul Newman and Joanne Woodward, and many others.

Katleman himself arranged the Newman-Woodward wedding on January 29, 1958. At the time, Newman and Woodward had not yet reached the heights of Hollywood

stardom and the El Rancho staff had to be advised of their status in a series of memos from the publicity and promotions office. One of the memos read: "Joanne Woodward and Paul Newman, Hollywood motion picture personalities, will be married at the bungalow of Mr. Beldon Katleman…EVERYTHING COMPLIMENTARY, PER BK."

Two other memos, sent out by publicist Gert Nolan, requested a wedding cake suitable for eight to ten people with the traditional bride and groom figures and the names "Joanne and Paul" written on it, as well as champagne, hors d'oeuvres, and Katleman's favorite brand of vodka, Zabrfka.

Obviously a very magnanimous man, it is said that Katleman was also a man of eccentricities and quirks. For instance, he never signed many contracts, even with highly paid stars. He was also sentimental, turning over the Royal Suit to a visiting couple from his home town of Sioux City, Iowa, when he heard they were staying at his hotel. The couple never did find out why they were given the red carpet treatment.

The resort flourished for the next decade, but on the night of June 17, 1960, Betty Grable and her husband, band leader Harry James, were on the stage in the cocktail lounge in an adlib comedy routine with a lounge entertainer, when a blaze erupted. No one was injured in the fire but the main building burned to the ground. Damage was estimated at $5,000,000. The cause of the fire was first thought to be faulty wiring, and then rumors started floating around blaming the blaze on arson. The sheriff's report only stated the fire started in the dressing rooms near the kitchen and spread from there.

Although charges were never filed, a man named Marshall Caifano was a prime suspect in the fire that consumed the hotel. It is said that Caifano was a Chicago mobster who became a high-ranking member of the Chicago Outfit criminal organization. A prime suspect in ten unsolved murders, Caifano was known as a volatile man, and was made overseer of mob-controlled casinos in 1951. It was his job to shake down casino bosses on behalf of the boys back in Chicago. Caifano was an original 1960 member of Nevada's "Black Book" list of notorious characters banned from the state's casinos.

Beldon Katleman had booted Caifano from the property just a few hours before the fire broke out, and the hoodlum had threatened Katleman. A *Las Vegas Review Journal* article states that on that fateful night in 1960, Caifano had been making unsuccessful plays for some of the resort's chorus girls and his boorish behavior was what prodded Katleman to ask him to leave.

Whether the fire was arson or just accidental, as firemen doused the last smoldering embers of El Rancho that fateful night, little did they or anyone else realize that the blaze would cause a legal conflagration in the coming years.

First reports were that Katleman planned to rebuild El Rancho in an even grander style than it once was.

As it turned out, however, the hotel was never rebuilt and the property became a motel operation that was a mere shell of its former self. It was this dismal situation that prompted Katleman to put El Rancho up for sale in the late 1960s.

Howard Hughes quickly seized the opportunity and negotiated a $7.5 million deal for it. Katleman originally agreed to the terms and accepted $2.7 million in earnest

money from the Hughes organization. Another $4.6 million was put in escrow at that time, pending completion of the deal. But before that happened, he changed his mind and demanded more money. The litigants spent two years in District Court battling over the intricacies of the original agreement. Katleman's attorneys attempted to dismiss the Hughes suit by claiming that Hughes had a "stranglehold" on the Las Vegas tourist trade and that acquisition of the hotel and property was illegal under the Sherman Anti-Trust law. But that didn't work and the lawsuit continued.

Eventually, on May 20, 1970, Hughes and Katleman settled out of court, with Hughes agreeing to pay Katleman $1 million over the previously agreed-to price for the hotel. Katleman's twenty-three-year reign as sole owner of El Rancho was thus brought to a close. He went out like the proverbial lamb after his lion-like entrance on the Las Vegas gaming scene nearly a quarter of a century before.

In an interesting side note, Tom Gregory had mentioned that he had smelled smoke in the house on more than one occasion. "I've smelled smoke twice in the back hallway and then one time in the main bedroom. And then one night I awoke with the sensation that someone was burning a fire under my hand. I felt like someone was playing with me with a lighter or a lit match."

Gary Cooper was a heavy smoker, but another possible reason for the smoke might also be Mr. Katelman. Could he still be angry about the blaze that closed his resort and is acting out in frustration?

After walking throughout the house, we all finally settled in the living room, and Tom told us more about the experiences he has had in the house.

Tom Gregory, the home's current owner.

"The house was being sold as a tear down," said Tom. The Coopers had it, then someone else had it, and then it was sold to a gay couple who said they came here one day and it was raining in the living room—and they are the ones who saved if from demolition. This was in 1996. And then we bought it from them and restored it, but the energy here is very active. And because it's very light and airy inside, it vibrates from the energy of the heat all day. The house, in my experience, is never quiet," he continued, "and it just seems to tell you what it wants."

The last time Tom experienced anything in the house was during an Easter party a couple of years ago.

"We had a lot of people here, about fifty in the yard, and I was feeling particularly down that day. And I remember walking back on the path to the little tea house,

and I felt like something just hit me. It felt like it walked right through me and that was just so strong.

"And then right before 911, I was sitting here in the living room watching TV and my partner was asleep in his bedroom, but I distinctly heard his footsteps walk down the hall and walk up behind me, and I felt him standing behind me. I was watching *Alfred Hitchcock* at the time and I said something to him like, "This is a great episode," and when I turned around to face him, nobody was there. I got up and went back to the bedroom and he was sound asleep. I was so freaked out that I woke him up and told him what had happened.

Tom isn't the only one who gets the sense that the house is active.

"We had a cleaning lady who used to get freaked out when she was here. You just have a sense in this house that

The living room fireplace, which was quite ultra-modern when the house was built.

it is someone else's house and that someone else's energy is eclipsing your own. I write about old films, I review old movies. I do feel sometimes that I'm drawing spirits in and I welcome them.

"Every night there is a loud bang here in the living room up near the ceiling. I think logically it could be because the house heats up during the day and then at night it bangs, but it happens even with it's cold and rainy as well and it's always the same intensity and pitch. If you were to stay here another couple of hours, I guarantee that you'd hear it. It's like somebody dropped a brick on the ceiling from about fifteen feet up.

"Being alone in the house is an experience and I never feel like I'm alone in the house. You get the sense that the spirits who live here are afraid that if we should ever

Orb next to the piano—which of Cooper's famous piano-playing friends has come back for an encore performance?

sell the house, which we have no intention of doing, that it would be torn down. It's like there's an overwhelming stress that the house is feeling right now because we're not currently living here. The house is stressed because it doesn't want to be left alone. The reason we're not living here right now is because it isn't a cozy house. It seems to have been built for entertaining.

Tom then pointed to a wall that was covered floor to ceiling with autographed pictures of Hollywood's most illustrious stars, many of whom were no doubt visitors to the house when Cooper was alive.

"The energy of those faces is undeniable; the energy locked in all those images. Each of those photographs is signed, so you have the energy of all the people who signed them. I think everything has an energy and rhythm. Since purchasing the property, Tom has become friends with Gary Cooper's daughter, Maria.

"A few years ago, we threw a party for her and some of her friends at the house, and Maria asked if she could bring her friend Pat Neal along to have a look at the 'new home.' She said Patricia Neal had never seen this house and wanted to see it. She and Gary Cooper really loved each other and, in a way, I felt sorry for the man because from everything I've heard, I don't think his wife was a nice woman. And because she came from a rich family, there was always the thing that she was marrying down when she married Gary Cooper. I don't think they got along well at all, but he appeared to love his wife and his daughter very much but I think he was a conflicted man because I know he loved Patricia Neal as well.

"Maria has said to me that she knows her mother and father are still here because she always feels them around when she visits."

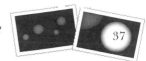

The wall of photos—a reminder of Cooper's friends from long ago.

Crossroads of the World

Crossroads of the World. Hollywood's first outdoor mall.

Crossroads of the World has been called America's first modern shopping mall. Located on Sunset Boulevard and Las Palmas in the heart of Hollywood, the mall, designed by Robert V. Derrah and built in 1936, is most definitely one of Hollywood's most recognizable landmarks.

It features a central building designed to resemble an ocean liner, an Art Deco facade complete with portholes, railings, life preservers, and decks. Surrounding "the ship" is an outdoor village of small, European-style bungalows in Italian, Mexican, Turkish, New England,

and French motif, hence the name Crossroads of the World. Rising above it all is a central thirty-foot Streamline Moderne tower, topped by an eight-foot, revolving globe of planet Earth.

Once a busy outdoor shopping center, the Crossroads now hosts private offices and has been used for location shooting in many films, including *L.A. Confidential* and *The Adventures of Ford Fairlane.* A reproduction of this distinctive mall can be seen just inside the entrance to the Disney-MGM Studios at Walt Disney World in Florida.

In the 1960s, the Crossroads buildings housed many tenants some of which were involved in the song poem music industry scam business. The term "song poem" usually refers to song lyrics that have been set to music for a fee. This practice, which has long been disparaged in the music industry, was also known as *song sharking.* It's estimated that over 200,000 song poems have been recorded since 1900, and the business of recording song poems was promoted through small display ads in popular magazines, comic books, tabloids, men's adventure journals and similar publications with a headline that read something like, *Send in Your Poems—Songwriters Make Thousands of Dollars—Free Evaluation.* Those who sent their poetry to one of these production companies usually received notice by mail that their work was worthy of recording by professional musicians, along with a proposal to do so in exchange for a fee.

In producing the recordings, the melodies were either improvised or recycled and musicians often recorded dozens of songs per recording session using minimal resources, often in one take. Some of the companies recorded new vocals over pre-recorded music backing tracks, using the same music tracks hundred of times. The recordings were then duplicated on 45 RPM vinyl singles or on individual cassette tapes, or were released on compilation LPs with dozens of other songs by amateur lyric writers. Copies were sent to the customer. Promises that they would also be sent to radio stations or music industry executives were rarely if ever kept, partly because the recordings would not have been taken seriously by professionals. The practice played off the desire of unsophisticated people, who often lived in remote areas, for fame and fortune.

Liberace's brother, George, was one such entrepreneur with an office at the Crossroads. Noted songwriter Jimmy Webb sold the rights to his classic song *MacArthur Park* to one of these con-men, and was known to sleep on the floor of his office when he was broke and homeless.

In the late 1960s, one of the Crossroads offices was occupied by a porn magazine that tried out young hopefuls by photographing them in the nude. It was here that an unknown John C. Holmes went one day and showcased his unusually large "endowment," leading to the start of his notorious career in adult films.

Needless to say, the entire Crossroads complex has housed a great many businesses throughout the years, and came into being thanks to the widow of a local political boss, Charles H. Crawford.

Crawford, who had been involved in many an unsavory mess, had his office on the site and was murdered there on May 30, 1931. Known as being a shady Los Angeles racketeer, Crawford's murder by a Deputy District Attorney was ruled justifiable homicide.

It seems as though it was easy enough to get in trouble in Hollywood during that era. It has been widely reported that L.A. mayors, district attorneys, and city councilmen took campaign money from madams, bootleggers, and gamblers. The LAPD's Central Vice Squad was on the take, and a loose, organized-crime syndicate was protected by the top aide of Mayor George Cryer. It wasn't violent, big-time, high-profile, Chicago-style organized crime, but it's said that its corrupting influence was just as real. By the mid '20s, Jack Dragna and John Rosselli, men with eastern Mafia connections, were engaged in a sometimes bloody rivalry with the homegrown, City Hall-approved Charlie Crawford for control of bootlegging turf. They also were setting up a West Coast outpost for the mob's nationwide horse-racing wire service.

At the time of his death, the portly, grey-haired Crawford was a financial backer in a new local monthly magazine called *The Critic of Critics*. The magazine's announced aim was "to rid the city of such persons as then Mayor John C. Porter, Rev. Robert 'Fighting Bob' Shuler, and to show up other long hairs who try for fame or money by limiting personal liberty of Americans." In ensuing months, the scope of the publication grew wider, its purpose less clearly defined. A typical article was entitled "Guy McAfee, 'Capone' of L.A."—an expose of the purported vice-reign of Former Policeman McAfee."

One of the magazine's writers was a man by the name of Herbert F. Spencer, a coast newspaperman of good repute, and six years city editor of *The Los Angeles Express.*

On the magazine's first birthday on May 20, 1931, Spencer was conversing with Crawford in the latter's Hollywood Office when a third man joined them.

Soon, angry voices, a scuffle, and pistol shots were heard, followed by a fleeing figure.

The shooting seems to have had something to do with a $75,000 bribe Charlie Crawford had paid to a man named Morris Lavine in some sort of bribery sting. The money, impounded as evidence, became the subject of a tug of war. Crawford asked for its return. Lavine also claimed it, presumably feeling he had earned the spoils of his crime. On May 19, 1931, clear title to the money was awarded to Crawford. The next day, David Clark, war hero, former crusading deputy district attorney, and current candidate for municipal judge, went to Crawford's office, the scene of the bribery sting, where he met with Crawford and Spencer. After an hour, witnesses heard gunshots. Spencer staggered into the street, bleeding and dying. Crawford's body was found in his office, where a witness said a policeman removed a cigar from the dead man's right hand. Judicial Candidate Clark disappeared for days, then surrendered, claiming that he had killed the men in self defense after they had tried to blackmail him. No weapon was found in Crawford's office.

After the murder, Crawford's distraught wife demolished the original building where her husband was shot and killed, and replaced it with Crossroads.

Because of the location's grisly history, I asked medium Michael J. Kouri to join me for a walk around Crossroads one sunny afternoon, to see if we might perhaps encounter the ghost of Charles Crawford.

As soon as we walked through the gate and stepped into the quiet complex, Michael picked up on three spirits.

"There is one that I cannot identify right now," he said, "but there is a woman who is dressed in clothing

that would have been typical of the 1970s. Her name is Veronica, and she doesn't want to leave. She is asking me not to make her go.

"Sometimes spirits think that when we're investigating, we're trying to send them away," he explained, "but I've assured her that I'm not a ghost buster and that she's free to stay."

"The third spirit I feel is that of a man, and he's over there around the boat. I feel as though he was strangled or shot and I feel that whatever he did, he deserved it."

We then walked towards the back of the complex and Michael came upon the spirit of a young man who claimed to have been shot in a gang-related incident there, in about 1987, over a bad debt.

I was hoping that as we walked around further, perhaps Charles Crawford might come forward, but instead, we encountered the spirit of a man who said his name was Richard.

"He's wearing a pin striped suit and is clutching a derby-style hat in his hands," said Michael. "I'm not sure who he is, but he's showing me that he had head trauma, so he was either bashed in the head, shot in the head, or something to that effect, and he dates back to the 1930s or 40s. And I'm also hearing screaming from a woman who is dressed in 1950s-style clothing. She's holding a pair of scissors, and at her feet, there is a man who has been stabbed many times. He's wearing a white suit and is covered in blood."

At that point, I wanted to find out more about Richard so I asked Michael to ask him for the name of his wife, thinking that perhaps the spirit was using a pseudonym, as many will and might really have been our elusive Mr. Crawford.

"He's saying, 'That old bitch? Why would you want to know her name?'" laughed Michael. "He's being rather aloof, but he's telling me that his nickname for her was Phoebe or BB and he's saying that he really doesn't want to talk about her because she was having an affair and he was really hurt by it."

Even though Richard was keeping mum about his personal life, he did have one bit of information to share, and with Michael at the helm, the spirit lead us out of the complex and down the street to an alleyway with a wrought iron gate which was adorned with barbed wire just a few doors down.

"He's telling me that this is where other people have been murdered, right through here. And he's also telling me that he was murdered as well, but is not sure why. He claims that she was having an affair and she claimed that he was."

Still wanting to find out who Richard might have been, I asked Michael to at least ask him for his last initial.

"He says, 'You can have the letter *P* which is an initial in my last name,' but I think his name actually was Richard Ellis. He's telling me that he's still here because he loved the place. He said, 'This is my home.' He also just told me that his best friend was Bela Lugosi."

At that point, we walked back to Crossroads and Richard either got annoyed at all of our questions or perhaps just became bored, because he stepped back to let a spirit named Dolores come through.

"Dolores is telling me that she was the maid of the couple who owned this place," said Michael, "and she is saying they fought all the time, like cats and dogs. She's also just said, 'I'm here taking care of the missus.'"

When I asked Michael to ask Dolores the name of her employer, she said, "I can't divulge that, all I can call her is The Missus."

"She was never allowed to give out any information about her employers," said Michael, "but she's also saying that she also took care of a Mr. Jenkins, and that he worked on this property and was the Mister's right-hand man. And she's whispering to me that she always thought that he was up to no good with the gangsters, and there were often lots of parties with men in pin-striped suits and hats who always wore red carnations in their lapel, but Mr. Jenkins always wore a white one in his. And all these people were involved with the Mister in his business, and his office was towards the back of the complex where the Tudor building now stands, and that's the area that he liked the most."

"She's also telling me that at one point in time, there was a car in here, right out in front, turning on a platform—not a car dealership, but more like an advertisement for a new car coming out. I asked her what year this was and she said 1930s and 1940s, and then just explained to me that she worked here until she passed away in 1959."

"She's been pretty closed-mouthed about giving out any more information," said Michael, but I think she's afraid of the spirits of the men she worked for in life, because they're around here with her. She's saying, 'In life, they threatened me all the time' and she's saying that she once witnessed a rape in one of the buildings. She had come into this room with a tray of champagne glasses, and when she saw what was going on, she dropped the tray which startled then men. One of them turned to her and told her to get out and not tell anyone what she saw or they would kill her."

Still curious about the elusive Mr. Jenkins, Michael asked that he come forward.

"Okay, I'm getting the name R.J. Jenkins," said Michael, who then mentioned that the initial *R* could stand for Richard, but the spirit then told him that he was not the same Richard that we had been talking to earlier, and this R.J. did not die on this property, but had a business here for a long time.

"He's telling me he opened his business here in 1935, stayed here until World War II, went to war, came back, and picked up where he left off. I think he was a florist. He's also admitting to knowing the other Richard but didn't like him. He said he was kind of a jerk, always putting pressure on people, trying to raise their rent, so eventually, R.J. left the property and moved his business down to Santa Monica Boulevard."

"I'm also hearing a man saying, "Get off my *$%&#* property. You don't belong here."

On a personal note, I've always felt that when we get a strong message from spirit like that, it's time to leave, and fortunately Michael agreed.

Although we didn't come across Charles Crawford that day, I'd say it's safe to say that Crossroads of the World is currently inhabited not only by living tenants, but also of the spirits of those from days gone by.

Chasen's

World-famous Chasen's Restaurant is now an upscale market.

The famous Chasen's Restaurant in Beverly Hills landmark was one of the best known celebrity hangouts for close to sixty years. The restaurant was opened in 1937 by vaudevillian Dave Chasen on the advice of his friend, director Frank Capra. According to legend, Dave originally concocted his now-famous chili recipe in Capra's kitchen and the director appreciated it so much, he thought Dave should share his recipe with everyone in town.

Chasen thought that was a great idea and borrowed $3,500 from Harold Ross, editor of the *New Yorker* magazine, and opened a little barbecue shack that he called The Southern Pit on Beverly Boulevard. It didn't

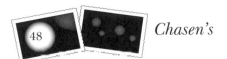

take long for the locals to fall in love with his fabulous chili as well as his Hobo Steak, and within just a few years, the wildly successful Southern Pit had metamorphosed into Chasen's, an imposing two-story complex where the vastly upgraded menu was served in a warm atmosphere of heavy wood paneling and red leather booths. The new digs also included a recreation room, a steam bath, and full time barber.

Over time, Chasen's expanded and eventually became an unparalleled haunt for the world's biggest stars and was also the site of the preeminent Academy Awards Oscar Party for many years.

Renowned for its long list of movie stars and other celebrity diners, Chasen's, like most celebrity eateries, had its special tables. The stars were seated in the small room to the right of the entrance. "Regular" patrons ended up in the back room.

Dave Chasen was known for being a kind and charitable man who took very good care of his customers. For example, when a pregnant Lana Turner had trouble squeezing into a booth, he had part of the table sawed off to accommodate her, and because Chasen's was off-limits to autograph hounds and the press, the stars felt they could let their hair down. Ray Bolger, who is probably best known as the Scarecrow in *The Wizard of Oz* would occasionally dance around the dining room, Jimmy Durante would often perform some impromptu schtick, and Frank Morgan, The Wizard of Oz himself, once climbed up on the bar and did a striptease.

W. C. Fields and film director Gregory La Cava could usually be found in the back, playing ping pong and needling each other, and the privileged were allowed to hang out for as long as they wanted.

Chasen's was the place where famed impresario Leopold Stokowski was introduced to Walt Disney and as a result, they conceived the Disney animated classic film, *Fantasia*.

Humphrey Bogart, John Huston, and Lauren Bacall used to meet upstairs to discuss the Blacklist of 1947. Alfred Hitchcock routinely fell asleep at his favorite booth, Howard Hughes often showed up with his own utensils and always ordered the same dinner—steak, mashed potatoes and ice cream. Errol Flynn and Humphrey Bogart would drop in for a steak. Ronald Reagan sat at booth No. 2 and would order boiled beef. The restaurant was said to be Ronald Reagan's favorite restaurant. He proposed to Nancy in Booth No. 2, and brought former British Prime Minister Margaret Thatcher there as his guest four decades later.

Although it was Dave's chili that made Chasen's famous, over time it was taken off the menu but was always available to those who wanted it along with their famous hobo steak and deviled beef bones.

Through the years, the restaurant's tales of Old Hollywood are legendary. Actors Peter Lorre and Humphrey Bogart got drunk at the bar one night and heisted the restaurant's huge safe. They rolled it out the front door, but abandoned it in the middle of the street. Elizabeth Taylor and Richard Burton got into an argument at Chasen's one night resulting in Liz throwing her plate of food at Burton and leaving the restaurant. The shouting match continued out onto Beverly Boulevard. Jimmy Stewart had his bachelor party at Chasen's in 1949, complete with two dwarfs dressed in diapers. Orson Welles fired John Houseman at Chasen's and threw a flaming can of Sterno at his former partner. A photo of Jackie Gleason

in the restaurant's office concealed a small door that opened directly to the bar so orders could be placed.

One evening in 1949, crooner Bing Crosby treated the entire Pittsburgh Pirates baseball team to Chasen's for dinner and it is rumored that Disco Diva Donna Summer wrote her hit song "She Works Hard For the Money" after hearing the line from a ladies' room attendant at Chasen's.

It is said that Chasen's bartender, Pepe, invented the famous "flame of love" drink at the request of bar regular Dean Martin, and it is also said to have quickly became Dino's favorite drink. The complicated cocktail took twenty minutes to prepare but was apparently well worth the effort. Frank Sinatra supposedly ordered sixty-five of the drinks one night for his guests.

A meal at Chasen's was quite pricey, averaging about $90 for dinner for two and about $60 for lunch but it wasn't the steep prices that eventually closed the restaurant. Newer eateries began stealing some of its thunder, attracting a "hipper" crowd, but Chasen's managed to keep going strong into the 1990s. Old-timers such as Frank Sinatra, Bob Hope, Gregory Peck, Kirk Douglas George Burns, and Jimmy Stewart remained loyal to the restaurant and some newer celebrities like Sharon Stone, Quentin Tarantino, Jack Nicholson, John Travolta, and Warren Beatty could be seen there quite often as well.

In his *Variety* column, the day after attending Chasen's final party, Army Archerd wrote, "Jimmy Stewart delivered the eulogy for Dave Chasen, who died Saturday, June 16, 1973. Chasen's, the restaurant died Saturday, April 1, 1995."

When word got out that Chasen's was to close, the onslaught of past friends who had turned to the nouveau

eateries began. Never had Chasen's done such a brisk business, but unfortunately, it was a case of too little, too late.

The original building was to be torn down and replaced by a two-story shopping center. But fortunately it was saved from demolition and eventually re-opened as an upscale Bristol Farms market. Before the market moved in, the site was used for private parties and as a filming location. In 1997, its illustrious contents, pictures, bars, booths, and even the paneling were auctioned off, but they managed to keep a couple of Chasen's original booths and some of the paneling, and the new tenants turned one corner of the market into the "Bristol Cafe" where hungry shoppers can still order Chasen's famous chili.

It is said that Elizabeth Taylor was so fond of the chili that, when she was in Rome filming the 1962 epic *Cleopatra*, she seemed to be having a bad case of "chili withdrawal" and sent owner Dave Chasen the following note:

"The chili is so good. All gone now. Please send me ten quarts of your wonderful chili in dry ice to 448 Via Appia Pignatelli.
—Love and kisses, Elizabeth Taylor."

Even though the original Chasen's doesn't exist and the booth where Ronald Reagan proposed to Nancy is now gone and Booth 2 has been replaced by the store's cheese section, celebrities continue to flock to the Chasen's site, this time as shoppers, not diners.

Because the building has such a grand history, I couldn't help wondering whether or not some of Chasen's old clientele might be haunting their old haunt and

asked psychic Michael J. Kouri to come along with me to explore the store and what little remained of the grand old restaurant.

We had no sooner pulled into the parking lot when Michael said he felt the presence of a late Hollywood actress Claudette Colbert, and he said she not only followed us into the market, but was seemingly leading us down the grocery aisles and right to the cafe, which is situated at the opposite end of the building. While there were no "live" patrons sitting in any of the booths and the tiny cafe didn't look open, the doorless entryway was not blocked off, so we walked inside.

A definite "Old Hollywood" feel was in the air and if you were to close your eyes and drink in the atmosphere, one could easily be transported back in time. It was almost like being in a time warp and the goings on in the crowded market quickly faded away.

Pictures of Danny Kaye, Frank Sinatra, comedian Jerry Colona, and even John F. Kennedy with a few cronies, all adorned in party hats lined the paneled walls, and potted palms sit on the back of the banquettes, bringing to mind the *I Love Lucy* episode where Lucy goes to the Brown Derby restaurant and spies on William Holden from behind a potted palm while he was having his lunch.

Michael immediately picked up very strong energy in the place.

"I feel a very strong presence of Frank Sinatra here." he said. "He knows we're here and he knows we're looking around, but it seems like he wishes that the hustle and bustle of the old days was here as well. He misses the Old Hollywood.

"Claudette Colbert came in with us, and she's actually standing right behind you over by those chairs,

One of Chasen's original red leather booths that was saved from demolition and now sits in the cafe.

and she's saying, 'Take a picture of me and let's see if it comes out.' She's also saying that this isn't where things really happened, and that her favorite booth was on the other side of the store. She's telling me that she really enjoyed coming here for lunch and that Lucille Ball, Desi Arnaz, Eve Arden, and many others would often be here as well."

I asked Michael if he could find out what her favorite menu item was. "She's telling me that it was the spaghetti and meatballs," he said, "and I didn't think they served that here, but that's what she's saying. She's also telling me that all of the 'old gang' still come here. Joan Crawford pops in and out in spirit, she says Jack Warner comes in from time to time as well, and in fact, I'm feeling Jack Warner here right now. I can hear him sort of yelling at

somebody. Even though this is just one small corner left of what was once a grand old restaurant, they still come back, but the other thing is, they're not just in this area, they are in other parts of the store as well, so that's kind of interesting, too."

I could almost hear a modern day shopper asking someone which aisle the pasta could be found on and hear them say, "Just walk right past Jimmy Durante and turn left when you get to Bing Crosby, then ask Jimmy Stewart to please step aside."

While it seems as though the reason for the restaurant's closing was because Chasen's had been unable to ensure its continuity by successfully updating its image and menu, and that may be the way of our modern world, for those loyal patrons on the Other Side who continue to visit the location, they may not be placing food or drink orders any more, but they're still in love with their old haunt and, it seems, keep coming back for more.

More Ghostly Urban Legends

Whether it be on movie sets, city parks, or in our own backyards, Hollywood has more than it's share of ghostly legends, and while I personally believe that spirits are everywhere, some legends are quite a bit more famous than others.

The 3 Men and a Baby Ghost

There is a scene in the movie *3 Men and a Baby*, the highest-grossing remake of a French film in North American box office history, where people claim to see the ghostly figure of a small boy who was supposedly killed in the house where the scene was filmed. There are also tales of other ghostly objects being seen throughout the movie, most notably a rifle pointing at the head of the "ghost boy."

That is the legend, but here are the facts: The scene in question was not shot in a house, but on a soundstage in a Hollywood studio. The "ghost boy" is in fact a life-sized cardboard cutout of Ted Danson (who stars in the film), which had been left in the background, presumably accidentally, by a crew member. This cutout is seen in full view in another scene in the movie as well.

There is no ghost boy. No boy ever died on the set, and no one involved with the movie was ever sued by the mythical parents of said ghost boy as had been widely reported.

La Llorona (The Weeping Woman)

The story of La Llorona is a Mexican folk tale that has been told for hundreds of years. There are as many variations to this story as there are people who tell it. The most common version goes something like this:

A beautiful yet poor young woman named Maria fell in love with a handsome and wealthy young man who recently arrived at her village. She took a liking to him and eventually they married and had two sons, but the man yearns for his other life prior to their marriage and begins to stay away for long periods of time. He is seen in the company of another woman, perhaps from his own wealthy class. In despair, Maria takes her sons to the river and drowns them to punish her unfaithful husband and then flings herself into the waters as well. Ever since, it is said that she appears near lakes and rivers, basically wherever there is water, and people who go near those places at night see her or hear her crying, "Ay. mis hijos!" (Oh, my children!)

La Llorona is a powerful presence in the lives of many Hispanics worldwide and sources claim there have been well over a hundred sightings just in the greater Los Angeles area alone. Here in Southern California the rivers have often been lined in concrete and turned into flood control channels, and in local barrios, La Llorona may be described as wandering the floor of the channels or the street and highway overpasses above them.

They say that the consequences of accidentally running into La Llorona include death, disfigurement, maiming, theft of your own child, and more, but more than likely, this urban legend is kept alive from generation to generation as

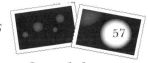
a safety measure to warn young children away from lakes, rivers, ponds, or streams where they may easily drown.

The Wizard of Oz Hanging

In the story of the infamous *Wizard Of Oz* hanging, a lovelorn male Munchkin is said to have committed suicide on the set of the film for an unrequited passion for a fellow stage hand who played the role of a female Munchkin. If one looks closely at the scene in which Dorothy, the Tin Man, and the Scarecrow make their way to the green Emerald City and meet the Wicked Witch Of The West for the first time, a man appears to have fallen or been pushed onto the background of the set. The figure has been seen rising and, according to some viewers, hanging from a tree and even swinging a little before being still. Some claim the figure does belong to an unfortunate stage-hand caught on set during filming, but deny the suicide. Disbelievers of the *Wizard Of Oz* hanging theory believe it is a bird spreading its wings—an emu from the Los Angeles Zoo. In fact, some peacocks and exotic birds were hired from the zoo and set free to roam on the indoor sets to give it an outdoors feel. The bird explanation is no doubt the correct one, as there is no record of a death on the set, but during the production of the movie, some of the actors were actually injured.

Margaret Hamilton, who played the Wicked Witch of the West, suffered a serious injury when her make-up heated up and nearly caught fire in the scene where she disappears in a cloud of orange smoke and fire. She suffered second- and third-degree burns to her hands and face, and it was later discovered that one of the key components in her sickly green make-up was copper.

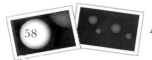

After Ray Bolger successfully lobbied for the role of the Scarecrow, Buddy Ebsen (originally cast in that part) quite happily stepped into the part of the Tin Man. Unbeknownst to him, however, the make-up for the Tin Man contained aluminum dust as a key component, which ended up coating his lungs. One day he was physically unable to breathe and had to be rushed to hospital. The part was immediately recast and MGM gave no public reason why Ebsen was being replaced. The actor considered this the biggest humiliation he ever endured and a personal affront. When Jack Haley took over the part of the Tin Man, he wasn't told why Ebsen had dropped out and in the meantime, the Tin Man make-up was reformulated from aluminum dust to aluminum paste.

Poor little Toto was stepped on by one of the witch's guards during filming, and had to be replaced by a doggie double for two weeks while she recuperated. Yes, Toto was a "she." Her real name was Terry, she died in 1945 and was buried in her trainer's yard.

During the haunted forest scene, several actors playing the Winged Monkeys were injured when the piano wires suspending them snapped, dropping them several feet to the floor of the sound stage.

The White Lady of Elysian Park

In the years right after World War II, it's been reported that some of the returning veterans were still filled with violent thoughts. One day, two young women were walking down Sunset Boulevard when two Navy guys drove up and offered them a ride, and they accepted. After some flirting, they decided to pick up some beer and cruise over

to a make-out spot in Elysian Park at 835 Academy Road in Los Angeles.

The area of Elysian Park is bordered by Silver Lake on the west, Echo Park on the southwest, Chinatown on the south and the 5-Freeway on the north. It is located next to Chavez Ravine where Dodger Stadium is located and home to the Los Angeles Police Academy. The park itself is the second largest park in Los Angeles at 600 acres. It is also the city's oldest park, founded in 1886 by the Elysian Park Enabling Ordinance.

As the story goes, upon arriving at the park with their dates, the sailors started drinking and tried to get fresh, but the girls resisted. After several failed amorous attempts, the two men eventually let the one girl go, but the other one was not so lucky. Not only did they rape and kill her, they also cut off her head. The murdered girl's head was found nearby, her body was never found.

To this day, whenever young lovers are spending an evening in Elysian Park, they always keep one eye open for the ghostly vision of the poor headless girl dressed in white, who comes back looking to find her lost head...or perhaps to claim a new one.

Ghosts of the Los Angeles Times

When tragedy strikes, do the ghosts of the dead still haunt the locations of their tragic demise? Some say that a few unfortunate souls remain at the sight of the *Los Angeles Times* bombing that occurred back in 1910.

From 1886 to 1917, Harrison Gray Otis was the owner and publisher of the *Los Angeles Times*. During that time, the newspaper pursued a strong conservative viewpoint, and was militantly anti-union in its editorials and in its relationship with employees.

On October 1, 1910, in the middle of a strike called to unionize the metal trades of the city, the Times building at First Street and Broadway in downtown Los Angeles was dynamited. The south wall facing Broadway Street collapsed, causing the second floor to also collapse under the weight of its machines onto the first floor. The first floor then collapsed into the basement, destroying the heating plant and gas mains. The building, with many of its workers trapped inside, was soon an inferno. There was a loss of life of at least twenty-one, and about the same number were injured, some of them permanently.

Some say that on quiet nights, people hear the muffled cries of those unfortunate bombing victims.

Monroe Haunts Westwood Memorial Cemetery

Westwood Cemetery is a quiet little haven that is surrounded by immense concrete and glass high-rise buildings not far from the UCLA campus. Quite a few big name celebrities are buried there including Truman Capote, Bob Crane, Rodney Dangerfield, Jack Lemmon, Dean Martin, Carroll O'Connor, Roy Orbison, Natalie Wood, Frank Zappa, and Marilyn Monroe.

On August 5th each year, a memorial service is held at Westwood Memorial Cemetery in remembrance of Marilyn Monroe, and people from all around the world come to pay their respects to her memory. But once a year doesn't

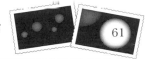

The simple plaque that adorns Marilyn Monroe's final resting place.

seem to be enough for the blonde star to be back in the spotlight because, throughout the year, Marilyn's spirit has often been seen hovering next to her crypt.

In addition to Marilyn's ghost, lots of other paranormal activity has been reported over the years at the cemetery including ghost lights, cold spots, and foul odors.

The Tragic 1901 Prospect Elementary School Fire

Hollywood Boulevard was once a residential street and, as the story goes, it once was the location of Prospect Elementary School. The exact location of the school has been reported to have been in several locations. Some say it was at the site where the reportedly-haunted Vogue Theater now stands. Others say that the school was located where the Hollywood Wax Museum now resides.

In any case, and according to lore, the ghosts of several children are said to haunt the Vogue Theater along with their teacher Miss Elizabeth, all of whom were burned to death during the horrendous 1901 school fire. But according to early records, there were no schools in Hollywood at that time.

In the year 1900, Hollywood was known as a small farming community with a population of just 500, many of whom were retired folks who had come west to escape the hustle and bustle of eastern cities. There were a few structures lining the empty streets; grain and feed stores, a post office, a newspaper, a hotel, and two markets, but no schools. It wasn't until 1903 when the city was incorporated, that the newly-formed city council passed a school measure, but even then, they were two students short of the twenty-four pupils needed to establish a school.

To solve the problem, a canny local real estate tycoon, Mr. H.J. Whitley placed an advertisement in one of the local papers. "Six months free rent will be given to any family having children of high school age who will come to Hollywood to live." The ad worked, and by September 1903, the new Hollywood Union High School, as it was first called, was in business. But as there was no school building available right away, the school took up temporary quarters in the empty storeroom of the Masonic Temple on Highland Avenue just north of Hollywood Boulevard, not far from the newly built Hollywood Hotel. So it seems rather unlikely that Prospect Elementary School ever existed.

The Ghost in the Elevator

B arry Shainbaum is an icon of survival and success. Today he is a renowned public speaker, broadcaster, and celebrated photographer, acclaimed for documenting some of the world's most famous and heroic individuals in his book *Hope & Heroes: Portraits of Integrity & Inspiration*, a photo-essay landmark giving witness to forty-seven heroes who offer hope and inspiration for the future.

Little boy spirit standing next to Barry Shainbaum, author-photographer.

On his radio show, *Perspectives with Barry Shainbaum,* Barry has discussed a myriad of topics with such distinguished guests as Ed Asner, Uri Geller, Monty Hall, Dr. Edgar Mitchell, the sixth man to walk on the moon, in addition to the taped interviews originally done for his book with Dr. Maya Angelou, Israeli President Shimon Peres, actor Martin Sheen and Dr. Phil McGraw.

I was a guest on his show a couple of years ago to discuss a cookbook I had written, and since then, we've kept in touch.

Not long ago, I mentioned to him that I was writing a series of books on haunted Hollywood and it was then that Barry came forward with a paranormal story of his own, then emailed me a wonderfully eerie photo of his ghostly encounter to prove it.

The photo was taken several years ago while Barry was alone in an elevator and here's how he explains the events that led up to him capturing what appears to be the image of a little boy spirit:

"This picture is very transcendent in my life," says Barry. "I actually took the elevator photo because I had a couple of shots left on my roll of film that I wanted to use up, so while going down in the elevator, I took a couple of pictures of myself. A couple of days later when I got back the 4x6 glossies, I was surprised to see the image of the little boy on the prints.

"There was a photo lab just down the street so I went in there and set up in the dark room and printed the photo up to an 8x10 and when I saw the larger image, I went 'wow.'

"The next thing I did was call up the owner of the building where the picture was taken and asked him if he

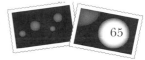

knew of anyone dying in the building, particularly a younger boy, and then explained that I had this strange image on my film. But I was told no, he didn't know of any deaths."

As he was telling me the story, I wondered out loud if the image might be someone who just happened to be in the elevator, or perhaps it was a little boy who was somehow attached to Barry himself.

"Someone speculated at the time that it might be the image of a child yet to be born," said Barry. "Or perhaps a spirit guide. But whatever it was," said Barry, "to me, that photo is proof that there is a spirit world. Because of what I had captured on film, I went back to the elevator a few days later and just photographed into thin air to try and recreate the image. Now this picture was taken about 10 years ago, before I owned a digital camera, and these anomalies were also present on the negatives, so the image wasn't something that came up in the processing of the film.

"While I wasn't able to once again capture the image of the little ghost boy, I did capture two disembodies faces hanging in thin air, one of a man and one of a woman who was wearing a beautiful old hat."

The ghost photo that Barry took in the elevator was not his first encounter with the paranormal realm.

"Up until 1985, all I ever thought about, as far as the paranormal was concerned was astrology. I'm a Taurus and every so often I'd check my horoscope in the paper, and at times, the forecast did coincide with what was happening in my life. But because I come from a strong math-science background where everything is proven beyond a shadow of a doubt, one could classify astrological readings as coincidence. Then in 1985, I was out having coffee with a lady friend of mine, not a girlfriend, in a restaurant in downtown Toronto, and in the restaurant there was a little flyer sitting next to us in the window from an astrologer upstairs who was running a $10 special. We thought "what the heck," and she and I went up there to see what the astrologer might have to say. She was a pleasant woman in her mid fifties with long dark hair. When we walked in, she looked at me and said, 'I'll take you first' and we went off into a little room for the reading. The first thing that she said to me, and of course she could have been reading body language, but she said, "The woman that you're with is not your girlfriend. I said, 'How do you know?' because it could have been a 50-50 guess, and she just smiled and said, 'I know.'

"So then she looks at my hand and talks for about ten or fifteen minutes and she seemed to be so accurate that it set me on an exploration—which for me entailed taking a couple of night courses, one on astrology and the other on psychic phenomenon.

"One night during the psychic class, we asked the instructor, who seemed to be was very psychic, how it all began for him. He explained that one day he tripped and banged his head hard on the floor, and within days, he began to see the invisible and to experience things, so the blow seemed to shake up his head. Anyway, in this class we were to do psychometry, which is the art of getting impressions from inanimate objects. We were told to take off our watches or other pieces of jewelry and put them in a hat so no one would know what belonged to who.

"A woman picked up the watch that I had put into the hat and said that the owner of the watch was a balding

older man. I put my hand up and said that the watch was mine. Because I was neither old or balding, several people in the class began to laugh, but I then explained that the watch had been given to me by my father who was in fact older and balding.

"During that period of my life, I was working in a school and was always complaining that the people I worked with were quite childish. One night during class, someone was doing a reading on me and she said, 'You work with children' and I said, 'No, I don't,' but she repeated once again that I did and I once again denied it. Finally she said, 'Let me rephrase it. You work with adults who act like children.' She was right and the fact that she didn't back down on her initial statement also gave me pause to think."

Barry had been suffering from bipolar disorder for many years and as says, "I was between life and death for quite a while, and I wanted to commit suicide. The odds in bipolar disorder is that one in seven sufferers will kill themselves. It's a terrible, terrible illness and the depression is so deep, but I knew from my personal spiritual viewpoint that I could not kill my soul, therefore I didn't attempt it and therefore I languished."

And as horrible as that was to live with, he claims that during that time, he had a paranormal encounter that not only set him on a search for the truth, but resulted in a spiritual visitation.

"During that period, I was living alone in an apartment, didn't take care of myself, and separated myself from society. I used to go to bed late with the radio for company, and one night at about three in the morning, I woke up to find a bright white light pouring into the bedroom. The whole bedroom door was illuminated by this light, and there was quite a bit of loud, nasty static coming from the radio. A second later, the light stopped and as soon as it did, the static on the radio stopped as well.

"I got out of bed and went into the living room to look out the window in the hopes that there was a very bad storm out there and the lighting was bouncing it around and reflecting in, but when I looked outside, it was a cold winter night and the sky was clear with twinkling stars. I thought to myself, "Oh my God, there is no explanation for this white light.

"Since this happened at around three o'clock in the morning and I wasn't going to call anyone at that hour, I went back into the bedroom, got into bed...and the moment I turned off the headboard light so I could try and get back to sleep, I heard creaking on the floorboards near the window. It freaked me out, so I reached up and turned the light back on and the creaking stopped immediately. I got out of bed and stood by the window but I sensed no presence, so I got back into bed, turned the light off again, and as soon as I did, the creaking started up again—this time right by my head. I turned the light back on, and the creaking stopped. I turned the light back off and the creaking began once again, this time coming from right by the window. I finally ended up just going back to sleep.

"The next day I spoke to an astrologer who was also into the paranormal and he said to me, 'Since you're not feeling well, you must have attracted a dark spirit to yourself. I can come over, and for $150, I will light a candle, do a prayer, and clear the place up for you. I told him to forget it. Then, when I went to bed that night, the moment I turned the light off, the creaking

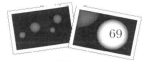

started again. Because I was so isolated by my illness, by the third or fourth night of this happening, that creaking sound became company for me. I expected to hear it and I knew for a fact that there was something there, even though I couldn't prove it for a fact, but I did hear it and this was not an issue of hallucination. It was actually there.

"After three weeks of having this happen every single night, it just stopped. And if I had taken a picture when I heard the creaking, it's quite likely that an image might have appeared, just like the little spirit boy in the elevator.

"When something like that happens to you, you cannot go back to the point before it happened. While we can't prove that there are other worlds, we have images, and I wondered at the time why it had happened to me...and I believe I was targeted for it; they meant for me to be conscious of other realities."

For some people, an occurrence of this nature would have been frightening to say the least, but for Barry, at the time, it was a comforting presence who might have been there to help him through that dreadful period in his life, to comfort him and enlighten him about the spirit realm. And in spite of coming from a scientific mind where things can either be proven or disproven quite easily, Barry said it wasn't the least bit difficult for him to embrace the concept of an afterlife and spirit world. "That surprises me because when a person experiences something like that and acknowledges it, you have to wonder if it's a hallucination, imagination, or the result of drugs perhaps, or just your senses playing tricks, but in my case, none of those things were present.

"I also recall an experience during my darkest days when I lived in a psychiatric boarding house for sixteen months with a whole bunch of sick people, and I met a chap there who was visiting one of the residents. We started talking, he told me he was a high school teacher and we started talking about the light and he explained that though he was a high school teacher by profession, years earlier, he was doing something else. He wanted to make a lot of money and he heard of people who were doing devil worship and became very successful at it. So he joined this group and they'd go to secret locations and conduct demonic incarnations and did very well. But in time, you have to pay your dues, and what happened to him was, he woke up in the middle of the night just like I had, but instead of waking up to a bright white light, he woke up with the feeling of a very dark presence at the foot of his bed accompanied by a terrible smell in the room. And when he looked down at his hands, they were bleeding. It scared the hell out of him and he made the decision right then and there and said to the presence, 'If you will leave me alone and not kill me or take me, I promise I will turn my life around immediately and will never do this devil worship again.' The entity then left, and this man turned his life around on a dime as the result of his visitation.

Barry has long since recovered from his terrible illness and for the past eighteen years he has been enjoying life to the fullest.

"My degree is in photography and because of my speaking about my previous issues with bipolar, I am now also a professional speaker, talking to mental health groups, schools, and companies.

"My book, *Hope and Heroes*, which came out in 2001, was inspired by my challenges. It features forty-seven

people from all walks of life who I feel have made a difference in life, many because of the challenges they have overcome. I have photographed and interviewed such luminaries as Nelson Mandela, Dr. Maya Angelou, Arun Gandhi, the grandson of Mahatma Gandhi, and Dr. Jane Goodall."

As the host of his own radio show, *Perspectives with Barry Shainbaum* on Faith FM in Kitchener, Ontario, Canada, and Hope FM in Woodstock, Ontario, Canada, he gets to chat with people from all walks of life. Topics include spirituality, inspiration, religion, holocaust, mental health, violence in school, pharmaceutical, global warming, the environment, the arts, and of course, mental health.

"It's a paradox that while I have my own radio show, I can't have a psychic or astrologer on because of the constraints of being on a Christian station."

When I joked that writing about his paranormal experiences in my book might be "outing him" to the public, Barry just laughed and said, "This has been a transcendent part of my life and I'm happy it happened. Things happen in wonderful and mysterious ways and I find it fascinating."

Hollywood's Legendary Haunted Houses

The Elke Sommer House
Benedict Canyon Drive, Beverly Hills

Elke Sommer, a German-born actress, who appeared in the 1966 film *The Oscar*, claims to have seen the ghost of a middle-aged man in a white shirt in the home she shared with then-husband Joe Hyams in Beverly Hills. Guests in her home have also claimed to have seen the specter. So much paranormal activity was reported in the house that the American Society for Psychical Research was brought in, and they verified the unexplained events.

Elke and Hyams moved into the house in Benedict Canyon in July 1964. Their first inkling that the house was haunted came just a couple of days after they moved in. Elke had invited a German journalist, Edith Dahlfield, over for coffee, and as Elke was pouring the coffee, her visitor mentioned seeing a man standing in the hallway, then walking into the dining room. When the actress went to check, she found nobody there. Her guest described the man as being husky, wearing a white shirt and dark trousers, and his features were so clear that she even told her host that the man had a rather bulbous nose.

Two weeks later, when Elke's mother was sound asleep in the guest bedroom, she woke up to find a

man standing at the foot of her bed, staring at her. Just as she was about to call for help, the man just disappeared.

Another guest who was staying in the house several weeks later, while Elke and Joe were away, complained of strange noises, a window that kept opening by itself, and a general creepy feeling about the place, especially when he entered the dining room. Whenever he went in there, the hair always stood up on the back of his neck.

When Elke and Joe returned home, they continued to hear strange noises in the dining room, doors and windows continued to mysteriously open by themselves, and other guests who stayed in the house continued to report the sighting of the man in the white shirt.

While neither Elke nor Joe had seen the ghost themselves, so many others had that they began to believe there really was something going on and called in Dr. Thelma Moss, a well-known parapsychologist as well as several other psychics, all who saw the same apparition. One of the investigating psychics predicted that there would be a fire in the house in six months time, but assured Joe that neither he or Elke would be injured in the blaze.

Whether or not it was a coincidence, a fire did indeed break out in the home as predicted, but the timing was a bit off. As Joe wrote in a 1967 *Saturday Evening Post* article, "Just after sunrise on the morning of March 13 (1967) my wife shook me awake. She whispered that she heard some noises downstairs and then someone pounding on our bedroom door. I picked up the .38-caliber revolver which has lain on our night table for the three years we have lived in our "haunted" house and got out of bed.

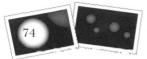

Downstairs I heard muffled laughter. Gun in hand, I unlocked our bedroom and ran into a cloud of thick black smoke."

The fire department was called, and Elke and Joe made their escape from an upstairs window. When the fire department arrived, they were able to quickly douse the flames which were contained in the dining room area, the same location where the apparition of the man was frequently seen. Interestingly enough, during an investigation of the fire, it was found to have started on the dining room table and the whole room was gutted by a fire so intense that it melted pewter plates and silverware.

Elke and Joe left the house that day and never returned. It was bought and sold more than seventeen times since Sommers and Hyams vacated the house, and many past residents have reported ghostly phenomena.

The Old Jean Harlow House
9820 Easton Drive, Benedict Canyon

Groucho Marx once said, "I'd have liked to have gone to bed with Jean Harlow. She was a beautiful broad. The fellow who married her was impotent and he killed himself. I would have done the same thing."

The man Groucho was referring to was Paul Bern, an assistant to Irving Thalberg at MGM. Harlow married Bern in May of 1932. Everyone believed it was an odd pairing in that he was twenty-two years older than his wife, intellectually superior, and was described as "a slight man, insignificant in stature, slender of shoulder, only as tall as a girl."

Despite his looks, he was known in Hollywood for his sensitive and compassionate nature, and many looked to Bern for advice, help, and sympathy. He was not into the Hollywood nightlife, and when he began appearing with Jean in public, it set tongues wagging.

It was soon announced that this odd couple was about to be married, and according to reports, their first few weeks as husband and wife were blissful. Then rumors began to emerge about Bern's financial problems and that Jean did not like the house in Benedict Canyon that Bern had bought for her as a wedding present. She wanted to sell it and he argued against it.

Just four months after the wedding, Bern was found shot to death in the house. His body was found by his butler in Jean's all-white bedroom. He was found nude, laying in front of a full-length mirror, and drenched in Jean's favorite perfume. There was a cryptic note laying next to the body which read, "Dearest Dear... Unfortunately, this is the only way to make good the frightful wrong I have done you and wipe out by abject humility. I love you.... Paul." A postscript had been added at the bottom of the note that said: "You understand that last night was only a comedy."

The official version of the suicide was that Bern had been suffering from a "physical infirmity" that made it impossible for him to have intercourse with his wife. The "comedy" referred to in the suicide note was Bern's attempt to overcome his impotence and carry out his marital obligations to Jean with a realistic, phony phallus. But why would a man with such an infirmity marry any woman, least of all a bombshell like Harlow?

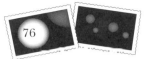

Surprisingly, this was not the most shocking information to come out of the inquest. It was learned that Bern had previously lived with another woman for many years, and the day after Bern died, the other woman also died "under mysterious circumstances."

It was said that Jean Harlow loved Bern so much that when his body was discovered, she too attempted suicide. Even though her attempt was not successful, Harlow's days were numbered. Five year later, she died from kidney damage at the age of only twenty-six.

Thirty years later, the house was owned by Jay Sebring, the premiere men's hair stylist in Hollywood. It is said that he loved the house but was always concerned about the fact that it was supposed to be jinxed. He knew the stories about Paul Bern's death, but he also learned that two people had drowned in the swimming pool. But he tried to shrug off the idea that the house was "cursed."

Jay and actress Sharon Tate were a hot item in the mid 1960s. Rumors claim they were engaged at some point, but their engagement was broken off in 1966 when Sharon met and fell in love with Roman Polanski, although she and Sebring remained close friends.

One night in 1966, Sharon stayed alone at Jay's house when he was out of town. She was unable to sleep and lay awake in Jay's room with all the lights on. She later told a reporter that she was very uncomfortable, although she couldn't explain why, and was frightened by every little sound that she heard.

Suddenly, a person that she described as a "creepy little man" came into the bedroom. She was sure that this man was Paul Bern. The man ignored her though and wandered about the room, apparently looking for something. Sharon threw on her robe and hurried out of the bedroom.

Sharon started down the stairs, but halfway down she froze at the sight of a figure tied to the staircase posts at the bottom of the steps. She couldn't tell if it was a man or a woman but she could clearly see that the figure's throat had been cut and was obviously dying from their wounds. Then the apparition simply vanished.

A very upset Sharon went into the living room to pour herself a drink but she couldn't find where Jay kept the alcohol. She felt an inexplicable urge to press on a section of the bookcase and it opened to reveal a hidden bar. Not thinking, she tore away a piece of wallpaper at the base of the bar as she nervously poured herself a drink.

By morning, Sharon was convinced the whole episode had been a terrible nightmare...until she saw the wallpaper that had been torn away from the bar. She was then convinced that she had indeed seen Paul Bern's ghost upstairs and had also witnessed a vision of her fate. When Sebring returned, Sharon told him of her ghastly, ghostly encounter.

Three years later, on the night of August 8, 1969, an eight months pregnant Sharon was living with Roman Polanski in a rented house at 10050 Cielo Drive.

Around midnight, on the orders of Charles Manson, members of the Manson clan scaled the hillside behind the gate leading to the house and made entry. The following morning, the maid made a grisly discovery. Among those found dead were Sharon Tate, coffee heiress Abigail Folger, her boyfriend, Wojciech Frykowski, and Jay Sebring. Some of the bodies were strewn across the estate, but the pregnant Tate had been stabbed sixteen times and lay dead with a rope around her neck on the living room floor. Graffiti found written in blood at the murder scene said, "Death to Pigs."

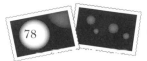

Was that scary night Sharon Tate spent in the old Harlow house truly a premonition of things to come? Some say the vision of Paul Bern's tortured spirit perhaps triggered the horrific vision.

A woman who bought the old Harlow-Bern house in the 1980s claims to have heard the whispering voice of a woman sobbing and pleading for help. Cold spots, ghostly footsteps, lights turning off and on by themselves, and a distinctive fragrance were also noted from time to time.

Recent investigations of the house reveal that the hauntings have settled down and that it's only the ghost of Jean Harlow who pops in every once and a while in a calm, gentle fashion.

After Bern's death, Harlow moved to 512 N. Palm Drive where she died a few years later.

The Hodiak Haunting
8650 Pinetree Place, Los Angeles

Anne Baxter is known as an Academy Award-winning actress, who took home an Oscar for her role as Best Supporting Actress in *The Razor's Edge*. Her first marriage was to John Hodiak, an actor who starred in several films during the 1940s and 1950s.

Hodiak died of a heart attack at age forty-one, while shaving one morning in the house he had built for his parents in Tarzana, California. He and Baxter were divorced by then and he was getting ready to go to the studio to film one of the final scenes for the movie, *On the Threshold of Space* when he passed away. Although Hodiak is interred within the main

mausoleum at Calvary Cemetery in Los Angeles, his ghost is known to haunt the residence that he shared with Baxter.

During the 1970s, an agent by the name of Hal Gefsky, lived in the home and Psychic to the Stars Kenny Kingston was privy to the haunted goings on when Gefsky lived there.

"Hal Gefsky had some guests staying at his house and one day when he was at work, the lady was doing something around the house. She looked out the kitchen window, and as she did, she saw a man with an old-fashioned man's hat walk by the window and he looked in and smiled. She thought he was going to walk around to the door and come into the house but he never did. So she went out by the pool and there was nobody around, and the gate was locked, so she couldn't figure out how this man had gotten in.

"When Hal came home, she told him that a man had looked in the window by the pool. He told her that that was impossible, because the guy would have had to have been ten or eleven feet tall, because the house was a two-story house and the kitchen was on the upper level. A person would have to go down steps to get to the pool. He told the woman that she had no doubt seen a spirit, but whose spirit he wasn't sure of because he said there were a lot of spirits in the house when the Hodiak's owned it.

"Another day, the houseguest was watching television and she screamed. It was a Saturday and Hal was home. He came running and the guest pointed to the television screen and said, 'There's the man I saw outside the kitchen window!' And he said, "Oh my God, that's John Hodiak.

"Before all this, Hal Gefsky didn't believe in spirits, but about six months earlier, I had lunch with Hal and a group of others at Cyro's. I said to him, 'There's the name

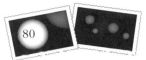

of your new dog.' And he said, 'I never mentioned the name of the new dog to you, so now I do believe in the spirit world.'

"Not long after that, Hal invited me over to his house and the actress Danielle Brisbois' mother was there that night. She needed to make a phone call. So she went into the den to make the call and came out in a hurry saying that when she picked up the phone, a man's voice said, 'I'm on the line right now.'

"Hal told her that that was impossible because there was nobody else in the house and he didn't have a party line. Then he gets a call a couple of minutes later from the guard who protected the property who told Hal that the alarms had just gone off and that somebody broke through the security system. Hal reassured him that there was nobody else in the house except the ones that were already there, and the guard ran down the list of people who were inside and named all of us, who, by the way, had arrived at the same time, so there was John Hodiak coming in to pay a visit."

The Barrymore Estate
6 Beverly Grove, Beverly Hills

Beverly Hills is quite the popular place when it comes to haunted tales and spooky stories. One of the most interesting ghostly encounters has to include the numerous reports concerning the Barrymore family, who produced a long line of talented actors and actresses. During the late 1970s, witnesses reported to have come in contact with the ghosts of John, Lionel, and Ethyl. Some of the more recent

tales involve a roaming specter that lost his life in a private cable car accident that took place on the property.

One odd Barrymore story concerns a cuckoo clock that was enjoyed by John. A friend, Gene Fowler, planned to position the nonworking clock's hands to the time of John's death when that unhappy event should occur. However, fate settled that for him. John Barrymore passed away one evening at precisely 10:20 pm. There was no need for Mr. Fowler to reposition the clock's hands. They already pointed at 10:20 pm. Coincidence?

Pickfair
1143 Summit Drive, Beverly Hills

The aptly named Pickfair home once belonged to Mary Pickford, a well-known actress in the silent-film scene, who was married to Douglas Fairbanks. The property was a hunting lodge when purchased by Fairbanks and Pickford in 1919. With massive renovation, the couple transformed the lodge into a luxurious twenty-two-room mansion decorated with ceiling frescos and the highest quality art and furnishings available. The property was said to have been the first private property in the Los Angeles area to include a swimming pool.

During the 1920s, Pickfair became the focal point for social activities and an invitation to Pickfair was a sign of social acceptance in the Hollywood community. Over the years, guests included such luminaries as George Bernard Shaw, Helen Keller, H.G. Wells, Amelia Earhart, F. Scott Fitzgerald, Joan Crawford, and Sir Arthur Conan Doyle. Fairbanks and Pickford were divorced in January

1936, and Pickford resided in the mansion with her third husband, Charles "Buddy" Rogers, until her death in 1979. The house stood empty for several years after Pickford's death and was eventually sold to Los Angeles Lakers owner, Dr. Jerry Buss, before being purchased by actress Pia Zadora and her husband, Meshulam Riklis. They announced they were planning renovations to the famous building, but later revealed that the house had in fact been demolished and a new larger mansion constructed in its place. The only remaining artifacts from the original Pickfair are the gates to the estate with their prominent *P* motif.

Pickfair is now owned by UNICOM Systems, Inc. as of April 2005.

After Pickford's death, numerous owners claim to have encountered her ghost. She has been described as wearing a white dress with ruffles and is often seen in the den located on the first floor.

In the beautiful entryway. Many claim to have seen a ghost who was thought to be Douglas Fairbanks.

The Keaton House
1018 Pamela Drive, Beverly Hills

Buster Keaton was an Academy Award-winning American silent film comic actor and filmmaker. His trademark was physical comedy with a stoic, deadpan expression on his face, earning him the nickname "The Great Stone Face."

In 1921, he made a movie called *The Haunted House* which seems to be a bit prophetic, since his old residence seems to be quite haunted.

During the height of his popularity, he spent $300,000 to build a 10,000-square-foot home in Beverly Hills. Later, owners of the property were actors James Mason and Cary Grant. The "Italian Villa," as Keaton called it, can also be seen in the movie *The Godfather*, as well as in Keaton's own film *Parlor, Bedroom and Bath*. Keaton later said, "I took a lot of pratfalls to build that dump." It was James Mason who later discovered numerous cans of rare Keaton films in the house; the films were quickly transferred to safety film before the original silver nitrate prints further deteriorated.

Keaton, who died in 1966, never built another house, and he ended his days living in a new ranch-style house in a comfortable neighborhood in the San Fernando Valley's Woodland Hills, but according to numerous reports, it seems as though his ghost is still attached to the home he lovingly built at the height of his career.

In Dennis William Hauck's *National Directory of Haunted Places*, Hauck says that television star Dick Christie is convinced that he shares Keaton's old house with the ghost of Buster Keaton who likes to play mechanical tricks such as unplugging the phone and turning off the lights.

The Crawford House

Christina Crawford heard voices of children coming from the inside of the walls when she was a child. She also saw them moving through the halls. After her mother, Joan Crawford, died, the wall behind the bed kept bursting into flames for no reason. Fire department investigators couldn't figure out the cause.

The activity started in the house while Joan Crawford owned it. She and her daughter reported hearing voices from within the walls. Ms. Crawford had the house "exorcised," without luck. Since then, the house has had a few owners, all of which reported some sort of activity.

In the book *Hollywood And The Supernatural*, Joan's daughter Christina is quoted as saying: "Not many people know that the house I grew up in may be haunted." She then goes on to describe "cold spots" in the home and ghostly child apparitions.

The authors claim the current (as of 1990) owner of the home had called in the Reverend Rosalyn Bruyere of the Healing Light Center to work on the house.

Bruyere says all the owners of the home, beginning with Joan, have had "terrible things happen...illnesses, alcoholism, addictions, relationship problems... and the walls breaking out in flames... in particular it's the wall that was behind Crawford's bed."

Furthermore, Christina says she is willing to believe that Joan's spirit currently haunts the house and that: "She was capable of real evil."

Bruyere performed an exorcism on the home and found the haunting existed on several levels, calling the home "...a place of conspicuous negativity... an 'Astral Central'...people have been tied up and tortured in that house... there is an area of the house where a child [not Christina] had been tortured and molested."

Bruyere says that spirits have been trying to burn down the home (hence the burning walls), but that since her exorcism, there has been only one recurrence.

Many owners later have found that the wall above the spot where Crawford's bed once stood has a tendency to erupt into spontaneous flames. The fire has occurred many

times over the years, and Kenny Kingston also has his own theories about the house.

"Joan Crawford came down with the 'Big C' and so did actor Anthony Newley, who lived in the house after Crawford. And," says Kenny, "while he lived in the house, he also lost $4 million because he invested his own money in the play *Chaplin*.

"I had Alicia O'Conner on one of my television shows that I did for Metromedia. She lived in the house at one time and she told my audience that she and her brother used to go downstairs in the middle of the night when everyone else was asleep to grab cookies and take them back upstairs to their bedroom. Until one night, when they had the hell scared out of them when three spirits appeared to them and told them that they shouldn't be eating sugar in the middle of the night. They flew back up to their room and vowed never to go back down there in the middle of the night on a cookie run again.

"Also, I was at a luncheon with Christina Crawford one time, and Christina told me that she thought that the house should be burned down because it's a very negative place."

The Gaynor House
Arden Drive, Beverly Hills

A ghost dusts the chandeliers in the old Gaynor House. Mitzi Gaynor and her husband Jack began to call her Mrs. Walker after a previous owner who died in the house. She often dust things that other maids have missed. The chandeliers can be heard jingling as the ghost cleans them. Two chandeliers fell from the ceiling for no reason.

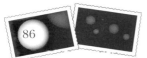

Additionally, a maid quit after seeing a stack of pillowcases rise up and fly around the room.

The Stanwyck Residence off Sunset Boulevard, Beverly Hills

B arbara Stanwyck and her longtime lover, actor Robert Taylor, continued to see and talk to each other after his death in 1969 at her home.

Another house, which the two used as a secret love nest has recently been the site of violent poltergeist activity.

Falcon Lair 1436 Bella Drive, Beverly Hills

B efore it was recently torn down, Falcon Lair was said to be one of Rudolph Valentino's favorite haunts. His beloved home was located in Benedict Canyon, which is rife with ghostly activity of all kinds.

After the actor's death, the house was auctioned off for $145,000, but for some reason, the new owner never moved into the house. Falcon Lair stood empty for eight years before selling again in 1934 for the ridiculously low sum of $18,000.

The ghost of Valentino has been seen wandering the property, touring the stables, and looking out his favorite window on the second floor. However, he does not linger only at Falcon Lair. He has also been sighted at his beach house in Oxnard, California,

at the Hollywood Forever Cemetery, in the costume department of Paramount Studios, and at the Santa Maria Inn in Santa Maria, California. Room 210 at the Santa Maria Inn has been beleaguered on occasion by mysterious knocking and an invisible presence that likes to recline on the bed.

Because he seems to be such a busy spirit, it's no wonder he needs to stop in at the inn for a much-needed rest.

Lucy's House
1000 N. Roxbury Drive, Beverly Hills

When Lucille Ball died during surgery on April 26, 1989, at the age of seventy-seven, she was still living in her home at 100 North Roxbury Drive. It was a beautiful, gray and white, modern colonial home, with large, rounded hedges out front. After her divorce from Desi Arnaz, Lucy continued to live in the house with second husband, Gary Morton.

Since her death, she is said to remain in the home and while the house has been completely renovated, the new owners claim to experience a number of strange happenings. They tell of unexplained broken windows, loud voices being heard from an empty attic, and furniture and other objects moving around inside the house.

Leeza Gibbons' Haunted Office

Vince's office, where a ghostly woman walked in to join us.

When I was doing PR for my first book, *Ghosts of Hollywood: The Show Still Goes On*, I was invited to be a guest on Leeza Gibbons' syndicated radio show, *Hollywood Confidential*.

The show's producer, Vincent Arcuri, had mentioned that Leeza thought there might be something going on in the office of a paranormal nature, so I thought it might be interesting to bring psychic Victoria Gross along with me to the taping to see if perhaps she might be able to pick up any activity in the Hollywood office.

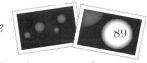
Hollywood historian Scott Michaels, who is a regular on Leeza's show said he couldn't believe that the offices were haunted because the atmosphere was so warm and welcoming and that Leeza put out such wonderful vibes. On the day we arrived, we found both those statements to be true. The offices are bright, cheerful, and Leeza and the rest of her staff make their guests feel right at home.

Vincent had mentioned that the building used to be an old age home in its former life, so I couldn't help but wonder whether or not any of the previous tenants might still be around, and the very first picture I took in Vincent's office revealed a rather pronounced orb.

While Victoria felt extremely comfortable in the cozy environment, she also sensed that we weren't alone, and Bobby Xydis, who was the first person we met when we walked in, admitted that when he was working alone in the office, usually towards the end of the day, he hears noises in the room just to the left of Leeza's office and also to the room on the left.

"Leeza's office is generally okay and I don't hear much coming out of there, but I do hear things coming out of the other two offices," he told us.

Victoria felt that in the hallway leading to those offices was a sort of ethereal dividing wall and the energy further back, where Bobby was hearing those noises, was much more intense than up front. "There's an entirely different type of energy in this hallway on both sides of this invisible wall," she told us.

Vincent mentioned that there had been quite a bit of remodeling done to their offices when they moved in three years ago, and because of all the electrical equipment in the office, Victoria felt that perhaps the high electromagnetic field could either be responsible for the weird feeling

people experience in that area, or for drawing in the spirits.

As she ventured back into those two rooms towards the back, Victoria admitted that she did feel as though something was there, and also felt strong energy coming from the floor below, but she also picked up a woman's spirit when we were sitting in Vincent's office just prior to my interview.

"I actually saw the spirit of a woman come into the space," said Victoria. "She just sort of watches the goings on in here." She also felt a very strong male presence around Vincent himself.

"He feels like he's one of your ancestors," she told Vincent, "like a grandfather or great grandfather, and he's a very protective spirit.

"It's funny, but the majority of spirits that are in this office are connected to you and Leeza and not to the building. But I also feel that some of them are coming from underneath and that's where I feel a lot of turmoil," she said, pointing down to the floor below, "and I feel like I just want to keep going in circles, and I also feel as though there's a male energy down there that's very angry. We'll have to check it out before we leave."

Leeza then came in to greet us and we were off to her office for the taping. But before we got started, Leeza admitted that she thought perhaps her own house was haunted as well.

"I've lived there for fifteen years, and nothing became apparent until fairly recently," she said. "Then, around my birthday, I was at home with my sister and sister-in-law and we were all together. We went into another room and saw a lit candle. This has happened more than once."

Psychic Victoria Gross and Vince.

In doing research on her house, Leeza learned that the home had previously been owned by Joan Crawford, Marvin Gaye, and the Nazi party, so no doubt there is a great deal of energy connected to the house.

After the taping was over and we were leaving the building, Victoria and I ventured downstairs to see if she could find out who the agitated male spirit actually was.

"A lot of times, energy gets trapped in buildings because of the Fung Shui, so it can make it feel as though there's someone hanging around," she began, but after taking a few more steps towards the area she felt activity in, she decided that there was definitely a male spirit around.

The courtyard, just downstairs from Leeza's office.

"There's a man here in the downstairs area and he's really in turmoil and seems to be quite angry. He's about fifty-sixty years old and his energy is transient. He's kind of scraggly, walks the halls down here, and I get the impression of a homeless man. If he wasn't homeless, then he comes from the time when this building was the senior citizen home, like in the 1970s.

Because the spirit was uncommunicative, we decided it was best to leave him in peace, and made a mental note to return to the building at a later date to see if he might still be around.

The Los Angeles Fire Museum

Old Fire Station 27 was opened on July 1, 1930, and at the time, at 20,000 square feet in size, the building was deemed the largest fire station west of the Mississippi. The first emergency response from Fire Station 27 came on the first day of occupancy at 3:14 pm to a two-story brick hotel at 6724 Hollywood Boulevard. The occupants of apartment 149 extinguished a fire caused by a cigarette with buckets of water. Since then, Fire Station 27 has served Hollywood, the motion picture studios, the stars who lived in the hills and along Sunset Boulevard, and during major emergencies, the entire city at large.

The Hollywood Fire Museum.

Prior to the year 1871, fire extinguishing in Los Angeles was done by the volunteer fire brigade, assisted by "peons" and water buckets. It was not until September of that year that any organization was effected. At that time, Engine Company No.1 was organized by George M. Fall, then County Clerk, who was elected foreman with membership consisting mostly of prominent storekeepers and property owners who assisted in carrying hose. The apparatus consisted of an Amoskeag engine and a hose jumper. This equipment was hand drawn until the spring of 1874, when the company became dissatisfied and asked the City Council to purchase horses for the engine. On their refusal, the company disbanded.

The era of the horses began in 1877 with the purchase of two horses for the volunteer company Hose Company 1 and ended July 19, 1921, when Water Tower 1, the Gorter Water Tower, assigned to Engine Company 24, was taken out of service and sent to the shops to be motorized. The Era of the Volunteers ended when The Los Angeles Fire Department went into service on February 1, 1886.

Today, a total of 1,101 uniformed Firefighters, including 226 serving as Firefighter/Paramedics, are always on duty at Fire Department facilities citywide, including 106 Neighborhood Fire Stations strategically located across the Department's 471 square-mile jurisdiction. Last year alone, the men and women of the LAFD responded 757,203 times to come to the aid of their neighbors in need.

I first visited Old Station 27 several years ago when the museum was still in the planning stages. I had an assignment to interview the personnel at the new Station 27 for a magazine article I was doing. New Station 27 is a state-of-the-art facility which had been erected a few years prior to my visit to replace the old relic next door.

While I was there, we walked over to the old station which at the time was in a state of disrepair, but the architectural integrity of the building and its huge, manually operated solid oak doors were in tact, as were the solid brass fire poles and copper ceiling tiles. An old brass bell sat proudly on one wall, a reminder of bygone times. Renovation had already begun prior to my visit with plans to turn the building into a museum, but the Northridge earthquake brought things to a halt. Then FEMA offered the city the needed funds to complete the renovation and the work got back on track.

Today, Historic Station 27, which has served as backdrop for countless films and television shows over the years, is a completely restored facility and represents what the station was like when it was in operation.

Because of the station's history and all the old artifacts it contained, I thought there might be a possibility that Old 27 might have a few resident spirits as well, so when psychic medium Mark Nelson suggested we spend a Saturday afternoon looking for spirits, I suggested we pay a visit to the old fire station.

As Mark, his wife Barbara, and I parked the car and walked towards the station, we could see that some kind of memorial was being erected in the forecourt. As we approached, we were met by one of the museum's docents, one of several retired firefighters who donate their time to the museum and work as tour guides and he was more than happy to show us around.

He explained that The Los Angeles Fire Department Fallen Firefighter Memorial is dedicated to Los Angeles Firefighters who have made the ultimate sacrifice. When completed, this will be the first memorial in the

Department's 120-year history that is dedicated to over 250 LAFD members who gave their lives in service to the citizens of Los Angeles.

He then walked us inside where three apparatus bays are filled with equipment, some dating back to the early 1900s and not to be found anywhere else. In addition, artifacts and equipment of all types are on display, dating from the 1880s through the present day. He explained that the museum also includes a Fire Service Research Library and a learning center where fire and life safety lessons are shared with both children and adults.

While the museum felt warm and welcoming, with all the ancient artifacts on display, I couldn't help but wonder whether or not some of the men who worked on these rigs

Lots of old relics here, and according to Mark Nelson, lots of old spirits here as well.

or spent many years of their lives at Station 27 might still be around in spirit.

Because this was to be a guided tour, with no chance of wandering off by ourselves, and the fact that when I asked our guide whether or not he thought there were any "firehouse ghosts" in residence, he kind of gave us a half-hearted negative response and then quickly changed the subject, I was relying on Mark's clairvoyant, clairaudient, and clairsentient abilities to pick up on any spirits that might still be hanging around.

"When I walked into the firehouse, my first impression was that there were three different spirits in there and one of them in particular was watching us very closely," said Mark, "and because there were so many beautifully restored vehicles and pieces of firefighting equipment, I kept hearing the words, 'Don't touch. Don't touch.' Then I sensed that there were a lot of men in spirit looking at us, and I think too that they were interested in seeing women in there because it used to be a very male-oriented environment."

Just a few steps inside the door stood a shiny red Cadillac ambulance which probably dated back to the 1940s or 50s, and in spite of Mark's initial warning from the spirits not to touch anything, I quietly suggested that he perhaps might want to lean up against it or somehow get his hands on the old vehicle to see if he picked up anything from it.

"I kept hearing the name Cassidy, Cavanaugh, or something similar," he whispered to me after our guide suggested we move on. "It was that sort of an Irish-sounding name. And there were so many spirits who had put time and energy there. There were several men who

Mark Nelson, using psychometry on this old ambulance.

died in the process of living and working there and I do feel it is an active place."

There was a small dark room, not much bigger than a broom closet at the far end of the room that our guide was very anxious to show us. It was the Hose Bay and he, Mark, and Barbara squeezed into the small room to have a look. I was standing just outside the door as the docent explained that this was the room where the firefighters hung their hoses. From my vantage point it looked deceptively small, but when Mark beckoned me in and I looked up, I was surprised to see that what the room lacked in width, it made up in height and was actually about two stories tall from floor to ceiling.

Mark was apparently feeling something in there and he suggested that I take a couple of pictures aiming up

towards the ceiling so I happily obliged. When we got back to my house and I uploaded the photos to my computer, there were two bright orbs perched on a beam about ten feet up.

"When I first looked up, I saw the spirit energy of a guy sitting up there," Mark later explained, "and he was sitting right up there on the beam where we captured the orbs. So the photo was good validation that something really was there."

We then went upstairs and were shown a display of firefighter's helmets from around the world, some quite ancient, then on to the old dormitory quarters, and the captain's quarters. I was snapping pictures all around and it was right in front of a display of an old hose that I captured yet another orb.

The hose bay orb where Mark said it would be.

**Another orb right above the hose.
All the old equipment seems to have spirits attached to it.**

As we were standing around in the hallway just outside the captain's quarters, listening to our guide tell us of future plans for the museum, I suddenly felt as though someone had given my bottom a gentle nudge and kind of lost my balance for a second. Could that have come from a playful spirit who just wanted me to know that he was there, or was it a polite way of telling me that I was in the way?

On our way back downstairs, our guide offhandedly mentioned that one of the other docents sometimes spends the night in old Station 27 and that he often hears strange noises, but they usually laugh it off. But after spending the afternoon at the museum, we all got the strong impression that when this guy spends the night, he is definitely not alone.

Ren-Mar Studios

846 N. Cahuenga Blvd., Hollywood

Ren-Mar Studios began its Hollywood life as Metro Pictures Back Lot #3.

The year was 1915 and Metro had sent a troupe of filmmakers to Hollywood to establish a West Coast studio. These movie pioneers found a small studio in the heart of Hollywood, surrounded by bungalows and orange groves. Over the years at this site, the company expanded, eventually moving most of its film production to Hollywood.

Ren-Mar Studios Entrance—very Art Deco.

In 1924, Metro Studios joined forces with Samuel Goldwyn and Louis B. Mayer to form MGM studios. The studio's logo, "Ars Gratia Artis," is Latin, and translated, it means "Art for art's sake." Later, in the 1940s, it was known simply as "Motion Pictures Studios."

The story of the Cahuenga lot is colorful. This was the place where they built big sets for silent pictures. Ramon Navarro, in 1923, swashbuckled through the palace of Louis XVI in the silent film *Scaramouche*, and in 1924, young Jackie Coogan floated on the studio's South Sea lagoon that was created for *Little Robinson Crusoe*. A few years later, in 1931, Jackie Cooper, along with the great Wallace Beery, broke hearts in *The Champ*. Marlon Brando marched around Stage 9 in *The Men* and Gary Cooper made *High Noon* there in 1952.

A virtual *Who's Who* of Hollywood have worked at Ren-Mar over the years, from Grace Kelley and Barbara Streisand to The Rat Pack. Robin Williams, Tom Cruise, Harrison Ford, Bob Dylan and Arnold Schwarzenegger have all felt right at home there in the shadow of the Hollywood Sign.

Stars of TV Land and television's Golden Age series such as *I Love Lucy, Our Miss Brooks, Danny Thomas Show, The Jack Benny Show, I Spy, Hogan's Heroes, That Girl, Make Room for Daddy, The Dick Van Dyke Show,* and many other classic television shows were created there. This was when the studio was owned by Desilu. Lucille Ball and Desi Arnaz started Desilu on the Paramount lot, but when they wanted to have their own studio, it was the Cahuenga lot that they bought, and kept it from 1953 through 1967 when Paramount Studios acquired all Desilu holdings. The studio has been owned and operated independently by the Lambert family since 1974. It has been home to

television, film, music video, and special event producers of a new generation.

In recent years, TV shows such as *Friends, The Golden Girls,* and the first four episodes of *Seinfeld* all called Ren-Mar "home."

Up until mid-1998, the studio was the headquarters of David E. Kelley Productions, the Emmy Award-winning creator of *Chicago Hope, Picket Fences, The Practice,* and *Ally McBeal,* all of which were filmed there.

Unlike the big studios, like Warner Bros. or Disney, Ren-Mar doesn't produce films under its own banner. It's a rental studio, leasing out their lot and sound stages to other studios, indie film-makers, TV shows, commercials, and even video games.

As far as ghosts and hauntings go, unlike Paramount, Raleigh, and Hollywood Center Studios, Ren-Mar is one haunted Hollywood location that seems to have slipped under the radar. But as we were to find out, the tiny studio in the heart of Hollywood does indeed have it's share of ghosts.

Victoria Gross and I visited the lot one sunny morning and met up with the studio's director, Carol Cassella, who has been at the studio for about twenty-five years. While Carol claims that she hasn't had any personal experiences of the supernatural kind, she has heard many stories from clients and other employees and after we walked over to the studio commissary, she and I sat down and talked about the reported hauntings while Victoria remained outside so that she wouldn't be privy to the reported goings on.

"We had a security rep who at one point was checking out an office building—that's what we do when people move in and out. She was going through the building when it was empty and she felt that she saw people out of the corner of her eye moving around. When she looked, there would be nobody there.

"On Stage 7, the air conditioning goes on and off by itself when nobody is there, and there was also quite a bit of activity on that stage during the filming of *Ally McBeal*. One of the actors, Peter McNicholl, had a bit where he would take a pitcher of water, tip it very slowly and the water would pour out very slowly from a high distance, and it would make a noise, and that's how he would get everyone's attention. He played a lawyer and he did it regularly in court, and Stage 7 was where the court set was built.

"One day when he was doing that, before the pitcher tipped and the water came out, the sound of the water could be heard and Peter just assumed that the sound man was playing a joke on him. He turned around to the guy and said, 'Very funny,' and the sound man picked up his hands and said, 'It wasn't me,' yet everyone on the stage heard the sound of the water *before* it was actually poured.

"On the adjacent stage, that used to be two stages, Stages 9 and 8, which used to be the *I Love Lucy* set, our guards still do something called a Fire Watch where they go into a stage hourly when there's no one here and check to make sure there are no fires. One evening, a guard went onto Stage 8 and just walked in without turning on the lights and he felt as though a curtain brushed across his face.

"Back in the 1950s, they would hang a curtain around the perimeter of the stage and put the set and the audience inside, and this guard felt a curtain that wasn't there and immediately turned the lights on and saw that there was no curtain there. It spooked him so bad he let his supervisor

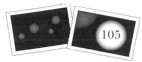

know that he would not be performing the Fire Watch again.

"When Calista Flockhart was doing *Ally McBeal*, her character had very messy hair, and one day she was standing on the stage and it felt as though someone was messing with her hair, kind of smoothing it down. She looked at the actor who she thought was doing it and asked him to leave her hair alone, and everyone who was standing around assured her that nobody on the set was touching her hair. 'Someone is straightening my hair!' she argued, but in fact, nobody was."

After hearing all the stories, Carol and I went outside and met up with Victoria and the three of us walked over to Stage 5, which was home to *The Golden Girls*, *Monk*, *Weeds*, and a 3-D version of *Terminator 2*.

Stage 5 at Ren-Mar Studios.

Because it was Good Friday and a union holiday, the studio was pretty much empty that day, and the stages were quiet, but Victoria picked up quite a bit of otherworldly activity and claimed that the stage was quite busy with one particular spirit man directing activity all over the place.

This stage was where Dean Martin, Frank Sinatra, Sammy Davis, Jr., and the other members of the notorious Rat Pack got together to rehearse for an upcoming tour. Barry Manilow, Neil Diamond, and Michael Bolton have also used Stage 5 for the same purpose.

Victoria immediately picked up a strong male presence that she labeled as "aggressive."

"He's not an evil entity," she explained, "but more like an old fart, and then there's a woman crying over in the far corner, dressed in period clothing from the 1800s, kind of like in a *Gone With the Wind* ball gown, but I think she's more residual energy than active."

At that point, Carol mentioned another psychic investigator had seen the male presence there before and said he thought the man had died there when he fell out of the ceiling grid during a production.

"That's not unusual for someone to have fallen like that because years ago," said Carol, "the lights were manually operated and this was before air conditioning, and it got very hot up there. The only thing that cooled off the area were these giant exhaust fans, which we still have on the stage. They would tie the men to the lights because they would pass out from the intense heat up there."

Victoria picked up quite a bit of energy on all the stages, but it was more like residual energy left behind by the activity that goes on during the course of a normal business day rather than spirit energy.

The dreaded grid where at least one man fell to his death.

The last stage we visited that day was Stage 8-9 which was where the Fire Watch and the *Ally McBeal* incidents took place.

Victoria and Carol walked in first, with me not far behind and as soon as I got into the doorway, I heard a man's voice say, "Hi!" right next to my ear. I turned around to see who was there, but it was only us females so I caught up with Victoria and told her what happened. She said that she felt a strong male presence not far from where we were standing but as she approached the entity, he moved away from her towards the back of the stage. She then took out her camera and aimed it towards the area where she had seen him go and took a photo. When she checked her viewfinder, big bright orb appeared in the shot.

I Love Lucy stage orb. "Ethel to Tilly. Ethel to Tilly."

"He's not the guy who said hi to you," she told me. "And I'm getting the impression that there is a young carpenter who works on this set that this older spirit is mentoring. I would say that this spirit is from the late 1970s or so and died in the early 90s, but he worked here for a very long time."

While I knew this was also the stage where *I Love Lucy* was filmed, Victoria did not, but as she was walking around investigating the space seeing if she could detect any other activity, she jokingly started saying, "Ethel to Tilly..." referring to the Lucy séance episode where Ethel dressed up as a medium to try and get in touch with Ricky's bosses' dearly departed wife. Coincidence?

When Victoria walked further into the cavernous stage, she got to one particular spot where she felt as though an argument had taken place between a man and a woman.

"Lucy and Desi were a combative couple," said Carol.

So perhaps Victoria was honing in on them.

After walking through two more vacant sound stages, Carol took us over to her office, which is more like a small bungalow or suite of offices. This was originally Desi Arnaz's office when Desilu owned the lot.

"This was the only office on the lot that had a shower," Carol told us, "and Desi lived here a lot when he and Lucy weren't getting along. In fact, there was an older man who came to visit me not long ago and he told me that he used to deliver for a nearby liquor store, and he remembers coming by to make a delivery one day, and when he approached the door, there was a row going on in here between Lucy and Desi."

The entrance to one of Ren-Mar's stages boasts a Hollywood motif.

Patio outside office building—Desi's office was just to the right.

Desi's old office getting an update.

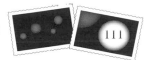

While Victoria told us that the office space, which at the time was under construction, was really quiet and she didn't pick up any spirit energy, I decided to leave my voice recorder in there while we continued our investigation in the hopes of perhaps an ethereal sound bite from Desi, but when I returned to pick it up a few minutes later, no EVP was recorded.

During our walkaround, Carol mentioned that she and many of the people who work at the studio felt very uncomfortable in the basement, that now houses the studio gym, so Victoria and I went to check it out.

You have to walk down a flight of stairs and then down a long hallway to get to the gym facility and, as we were walking down the hall, Victoria mentioned that because there were a lot of electrical boxes and such in the hallway, the spirits that were down in that area would be made stronger by the electrical energy.

Down in the basement orb where employees fear to tread.

Going back up into the light.

Once we reached the gym, Victoria said she felt quite a bit of turmoil at one spot right next to the door.

"I just got very lightheaded here," she said, "and I feel like someone just knocked me against the wall. There's something right here that happened and I feel as though someone is banging me against the wall." A moment later, she grabbed her chest and said it felt as though she had just been punched and actually had to sit down on a nearby bench and get out of that energy for a moment to get her bearings back. "I'd say that this altercation happened sometime in the late 40s to early 50s."

Because she felt so uncomfortable down there, we decided to leave the basement and head back upstairs.

It was Victoria's consensus that there was probably a great deal more activity, especially in the offices, at night, so we will set up a date to come back to Ren-Mar someday after dark.

Victoria picking up some negative residual energy.

Ice Age Ghosts?

The George C. Page Museum
5801 Wilshire Boulevard, Los Angeles

The George C. Page Museum in Rancho LaBrea, is just a few steps away from The La Brea Tar Pits in Hancock Park. Hancock Park is situated within urban Los Angeles, near the Miracle Mile district and is part of the Natural History Museum of Los Angeles County. It is one of the world's most famous fossil sites and features the largest and most diverse assemblage of extinct Ice Age plants and animals. Visitors learn about Los Angeles as it was during the last Ice Age, 10,000 and 40,000 years ago, when animals such as saber-toothed cats and mammoths roamed the Los Angeles Basin. Through windows at the Fossil Preparation Laboratory, visitors watch bones being cleaned and repaired while, outside the museum, the twenty-three acres of Hancock Park feature observation pits and life-size replicas of some of the extinct mammals.

In Hancock Park, asphalt, colloquially termed tar, seeps up from underground. The asphalt is derived from petroleum deposits which originate from underground locations throughout the Los Angeles Basin. The asphalt reaches the surface at several locations in the park, forming pools. Methane gas also seeps up, causing bubbles which makes the asphalt appear to boil. Asphalt and methane also appear under surrounding buildings, requiring special operations to remove it periodically, lest it weaken the

buildings' foundations. It was recently discovered that the bubbles are caused by hardy forms of bacteria embedded in the natural asphalt that are eating away at the petroleum and releasing methane; of the bacteria sampled so far, about 200 to 300 are previously unknown species.

This seepage has been happening for tens of thousands of years. From time to time, the asphalt would form a pool deep enough to trap animals, and the surface would be covered with a layer of water, dust, and leaves. Animals would wander in, become trapped and eventually die. Predators would also enter to eat the trapped animals, and themselves become stuck.

As the bones of the dead animals sank into the asphalt, it fossilized them, turning them a dark brown or black color. Lighter fractions of petroleum evaporated from the asphalt, leaving a more solid substance which held the bones. Apart from the dramatic fossils of large mammals, the asphalt also preserved very small "microfossils," wood and plant remnants, and even pollen grains. Radiometric dating of preserved wood and bones has given an age of 38,000 years for the oldest known material from the La Brea seeps, and they are still ensnaring organisms today.

Fossils have been excavated from hundreds of the pits in the park. Work started in the early twentieth century. In the 1940s and 1950s, there was great public excitement over the dramatic mammal fossils recovered. By the 2000s, attention had shifted to microfossils, to fossilized insects and plants, and even to pollen grains. These fossils help define a picture of what is thought to be a cooler, moister climate present in the Los Angeles basin during the glacial age.

There are saber-toothed cat and giant sloth models on display at the La Brea Tar Pits Museum. Among the prehistoric species associated with the La Brea Tar Pits are

mammoths, dire wolves, short-faced bears, ground sloths, and the state fossil of California, the saber-toothed cat, Smilodon californicus. Only one human has ever been found, a partial skeleton of a Native American woman, dated at approximately 9,000 BC. Much of the early work in identifying species was performed in the early twentieth century by John C. Merriam of the University of California.

It is said that George C. Page came to southern California because of an orange. The orange tasted so sweet to the boy in rural Nebraska, that when he left home at age sixteen, he headed west to the "Land of Sunshine." The orange became the inspiration for Page's first company, Mission Pak, which specialized in packaging and mailing California fruits to people in colder climates. The seasonal nature of the business enabled Page to found a successful sports car manufacturing plant and to develop industrial parks, residential areas, and other real estate projects.

Page established his pattern of philanthropy over forty years ago by building a youth center in Hawthorne, California, and provided major donations to both public and private institutions. His early fascination with the unique La Brea asphalt deposits prompted him to build the museum.

I've always been fascinated by the Tar Pits and wondered if Victoria Gross might be able to pick up a few humans along with the animal spirits that haunt the site. It seemed to me that perhaps some unwitting soul may have fallen into the tar pits at some time or another and I was wondering if they might still be around.

This idea came to mind one day when I was reading about an excavation that took place in the tar pits at the beginning of the twentieth century. It said, in part, that the only prehistoric human remains uncovered in the Rancho La Brea area were those of the *La Brea Woman*, found in

1914. Excavators uncovered a woman's skull and partial skeleton. La Brea Woman had died about 9,000 years ago. She was believed to have been about 18-24 years old and stood about 4 feet 8-10 inches (1.5 meters) tall. Wear on her surviving teeth indicated a diet of stone-ground meal. Her skull structure indicates that she was of the Chumash people. Speaking of her skull, it was found fractured, suggesting a blow to the head that may have killed her. She might just be L.A.'s first known case of homicide.

The museum used to have an exhibit devoted entirely to La Brea Woman until just a few years ago, when the curator decided to remove it amid concerns of offending local Native Americans. Other reports indicate that after re-testing the bones, she may not have been either quite as old as was originally reported and not part of the tribe that lived in the environs of the tar pits, where she ended up. Where she came from, who she really was, and how old she is is now is anybody's guess. In any case, she is now tucked away safely with the museum archives, and doesn't seem to be haunting the place of her death.

After a quick walkaround, Victoria didn't pick up any entities anywhere near the sticky goo, but she was drawn to the Page Museum just a few feet away. The museum was about to close but we had time to go into the gift shop and had a look around. Strangely enough, it was there that Victoria picked up the spirit of a man in the shop, so she asked the guy behind the counter if he ever felt as though there were any ghosts around.

He said that he didn't feel anything in the gift shop itself, but mentioned that there were places inside the museum that felt a bit haunted. Because it was closing time, he couldn't take us through that day, but we made arrangements to come back again and check it out.

The Streets Are "Alive" with Ghosts

Whether people realize it or not, there's a lot more activity going around us all the time than what the eyes and ears can perceive. There is a whole other dimension coexisting alongside the real world and even though most people aren't privy to it, those on the other side are still very much "alive."

The Corner of Wilshire and Fairfax

This busy intersection made the news when rapper Notorious B.I.G. was shot to death on March 9, 1997, by an unknown assailant in a drive-by shooting.

When Biggie debuted with the 1994 record *Ready to Die*, he was a central figure in the East Coast and increased New York's viability at a time when hip hop was mostly dominated by West Coast artists. The following year, Biggie led his childhood friends to chart success through his protégé group, Junior M.A.F.I.A.

While recording his second album, Biggie was heavily involved in the East Coast-West Coast hip hop feud dominating the scene at the time

In the early morning hours, he was leaving a party at the Peterson Automotive Museum that was thrown by *Vibe* magazine in celebration of the Soul Train Music Awards. He sat in the passenger side of his SUV, with his bodyguard in the driver's seat and Junior M.A.F.I.A. member Lil'

The famous corner of Hollywood and Vine.

Cease in the back. According to most witnesses, another vehicle pulled up on the right side of the SUV while it was stopped at a red light, and six to ten shots were fired. Biggie's bodyguard rushed him to the nearby Cedars-Sinai Medical Center, but it was already too late.

While no active hauntings have been reported at this busy intersection, places where violent deaths occur are often quite active, so perhaps a visit to the site in the wee hours of the morning when traffic is not so heavy should be put on my "To Do" list.

The Viper Room
8852 Sunset Boulevard
on the Sunset Strip

This is the location where actor River Phoenix collapsed and died of a drug overdose on the pavement outside of this club on Halloween night 1993. He was twenty-three years old.

The Viper Room, once co-owned by actor Johnny Depp, has recently been sold to Harry Morton, son of Hard Rock Café founder Peter Morton. Before it was the Viper Room, the club was first known as the Melody Room, and then Filthy McNasty's. In fact, if you've seen the movie *The Doors*, they pan past Filthy's in the opening segment.

I'm quite sure the ghost of River Phoenix does not hang out in front of the old Viper Room 24/7, but I wouldn't be surprised if he stops by on All Hallows Eve to acknowledge all the folks who go there on that night to pay their respects.

The Viper Room today.

Memorial sign for River Phoenix. *Courtesy of Lisa Burks*

The Black Dahlia
3800 block of South Norton Avenue

On January 15, 1947, Elizabeth Short's body was discovered on a vacant lot of the 3800 block of South Norton Avenue in the Leimert Park neighborhood of Los Angeles. Her body was cut in half at the waist and mutilated.

Houses were built on the property and the location of where Short's body was found is now part of a well-manicured lawn. The current residents have not mentioned any reported sightings of Elizabeth Short's ghost, but the residual energy in that area is very strong.

Grauman's Chinese Theater
6925 Hollywood Boulevard

Victor Killian was a character actor of gruff demeanor who played in dozens of films through the thirties and forties. He gained perhaps his greatest fame, as the title character's libidinous grandfather on the *Mary Hartman, Mary Hartman* TV series. In 1982, the actor was beaten to death by robbers burglarizing his apartment at 6500 Yucca Street, and it is said that his ghost walks up and down in front of the Chinese Theater searching for the man who bludgeoned him to death.

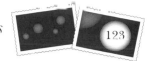

The world-famous Chinese Theater.

Intersection of Beverly Glen and Santa Monica Boulevard

Comedian Ernie Kovacs died tragically in an automobile accident on January 13, 1962, just ten days before his forty-third birthday. After meeting his wife, Edie Adams, at a party hosted by Milton Berle and his wife, the couple left in separate cars—Kovacs had been working for much of the evening before the party and, during an unusual southern California rainstorm, the comedian lost control of his Chevrolet Corvair station wagon while turning too fast, crashing into a power pole at the corner of Beverly Glen and Santa Monica Boulevards. He was being thrown halfway out the passenger side, dying almost instantly from chest and head injuries.

Rumors suggested Kovacs lost control of the car while trying to light a cigar. A photographer managed to arrive moments later, and morbid images of Kovacs in death appeared in newspapers across the United States. Years later, in a documentary about Kovacs, Edie Adams revealed she telephoned the coroner's office impatiently when she learned of the crash, and an official cupped the telephone, saying to a colleague it was "Mrs. Kovacs" and what should he tell her? She became inconsolable upon the confirmation. Jack Lemmon, who also attended the Berle party, identified Kovacs' body at the morgue when Adams became too overcome to do it.

Because Kovacs was the consummate jokester, it wouldn't surprise me in the least if people passing the

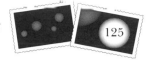
site get a whiff of his trademark cigar every now and then—a not-so-subtle message from a not-so-subtle comedian.

404-B South Alvarado

This is the former site of the Alvarado Court Apartments, near MacArthur Park, where on February 1, 1922, Paramount film director William Desmond Taylor, was shot to death in his bungalow.

At 7:30 am on the morning of February 2, 1922, the body of William Desmond Taylor was found inside his bungalow at the *Alvarado Court Apartments*, 404-B South Alvarado Street, in the Westlake Park area of downtown Los Angeles, California, which was then known as a trendy and affluent neighborhood. A crowd gathered inside and someone identifying himself as a doctor stepped forward, made a cursory examination of the body, declared the victim had died of a stomach hemorrhage and was never seen again—perhaps out of embarrassment, because sometime later doubts arose. In Taylor's pockets were a wallet holding $78, a silver cigarette case, a Waltham pocket watch and an ivory toothpick. A two carat diamond ring was on his finger. A large but undetermined sum of cash which Taylor had shown to his accountant the day before was missing and apparently never accounted for. After some investigation, the time of Taylor's death was set at 7:50 in the evening of February 1, 1922.

More than a dozen individuals were eventually named as suspects by both the press and the police. Newspaper reports at the time were both overwhelmingly

sensationalized and speculative, even fabricated, and the murder was used as the basis for much subsequent "true crime" fiction. Many inaccuracies were carried forward by later writers who used articles from the popular press as their sources. Overall, most accounts have consistently focused on seven people as suspects and witnesses.

It was one of the biggest crimes to hit Hollywood and the murder mystery dominated the headlines of the period. The list of suspects included many showbiz figures, including silent film actress Mabel Normand (Mack Sennett's leading lady), but the case remains unsolved to this day. The site is a parking lot now, and the once wealthy neighborhood is now shabby.

Taylor is buried at the Hollywood Forever Cemetery, but chances are, his restless spirit still returns to the scene of the crime looking for justice.

Basin C in Marina Del Rey

Beach Boys drummer Dennis Wilson drowned December 28, 1983, while swimming under his boat, Emerald, that was docked in the Marina.

He had been diving off the boat slip searching for personal belongings that had fallen or been tossed overboard during the years he'd docked his sailboat there. Plagued by drug and alcohol abuse during his adult life, an autopsy showed that he was drunk at the time of his death. He was 39 years old.

One can't help but wonder whether Dennis' spirit shows up near the slip where his boat was docked, or perhaps underwater, still searching for his lost belongings.

The Intersection of Yucca and Cherokee

Actor Percy Kilbride was a popular character actor, probably best known as Pa Kettle in the popular *Ma and Pa Kettle* series of movies.

In later years, the actor suffered from Alzheimer's disease, and in the fall of 1964, he and actor friend Ralf Belmont were crossing at the intersection at Yucca and Cherokee in Hollywood near his home, on the way to his morning walk down Hollywood Boulevard, when both men were struck by a speeding car. Belmont was killed instantly, but Percy survived and was taken to a Los Angeles Hospital where he underwent brain surgery. He lingered for over a week but finally succumbed to pneumonia and his injuries at age seventy-six. It is said that his ghost still takes a morning walk down the boulevard and lingers at the intersection where the vehicle took his life.

Scott in Wonderland

The Wonderland Murders, also known as Four on the Floor or Laurel Canyon Murders, occurred at 8763 Wonderland Avenue in the Laurel Canyon area of the Hollywood Hills in 1981, when four people were beaten to death with a steel pipe in a drug-related plot that involved "larger-than-life" porn star John Holmes. The crime was allegedly masterminded by businessman, drug dealer, and reputed gangster Eddie Nash who was a Los Angeles nightclub and restaurant owner.

The Wonderland Gang was comprised of three people, Joy Audrey Gold Miller, William R. DeVerell (Miller and DeVerell were a couple), and their leader Ronald Launius, who were all reputed drug users and dealers. They lived in a rented house at 8763 Wonderland Avenue.

On June 28, 1981, the trio got together with two other unsavory types, David Lind and Tracy McCourt, and also John Holmes, who used to buy drugs from them. During their visit, the group decided to rob the home of wealthy Eddie Nash (aka Adel Nasrallah) who reportedly was also in the drug trade.

Shortly thereafter, Holmes paid a visit to his friend Nash on the guise of buying drugs. While he was there, Holmes scouted out the house and managed to unlock a back door without Nash's knowledge. The next morning DeVerell, Lanius, Lind, and McCourt went to Nash's house. While McCourt stayed in the car, a stolen Ford Granada, the other three entered through the previously unlocked door. They took Nash and his live-in bodyguard, Gregory DeWitt Diles, by surprise and handcuffed them. Then,

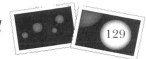

Site of the Wonderland Murders in haunted Laurel Canyon.

after looting the house of money, drugs, and jewelry, the group fled the scene and returned to Wonderland Avenue to split up the loot, shortchanging Holmes and McCourt in the process.

Nash suspected that Holmes had been involved in the robbery, and after he managed to free himself and his bodyguard, he ordered Diles to go get Holmes and bring him to back to the house. The porn star was found on the street in Hollywood, wearing one of Nash's stolen rings.

Nash had Diles beat up Holmes until he identified the people behind the crime. This beating was witnessed by Scott Thorson, then-boyfriend of Liberace, who, at the time, happened to be picking up drugs at Nash's house.

In the early morning hours of July 1, 1981, two days after the robbery and the day after Holmes' confession, Miller, DeVerell, Launius, Launius' wife, Susan, and Barbara Richardson (Lind's girlfriend) were bludgeoned repeatedly with striated steel pipes. Susan Launius survived with serious injuries, but the other four were killed. Veteran LAPD detectives who arrived at the house after the murders claimed they had never seen so much blood at one crime scene.

John Holmes was present at the murder site, as evidenced by his finger prints, but it is unknown whether he actually participated in any of the killings.

According to court testimony, David Lind managed to survive the attack because he had spent the night at a San Fernando Valley motel, consuming drugs with a prostitute. Shortly after the news media reported the murders, Lind contacted the police and pointed the finger at Nash and Holmes. LAPD detectives Tom Lange and Robert Souza,

who were to work on the O.J. Simpson murder case thirteen years later, lead the murder investigation.

When police searched Nash's home they found more than a million dollars in cocaine and Nash ended up spending two years in prison. Holmes was charged with the murders but his lawyer, Earl Hanson, successfully presented Holmes as one of the victims, and Holmes was acquitted on June 16, 1982. He refused to testify and cooperate with authorities and spent some time in jail for contempt of court.

Because the Wonderland Murders have been described as one of the bloodiest mass murders in California history and it's been said that the tormented spirits of the murder victims still remain, perhaps trying to avenge their horrible deaths, it's often been thought that the site is still very haunted by the victims who died there in 1981.

Leave it to Hollywood historian and owner of Dearly Departed Tours, Scott Michaels, to go up to the Wonderland house to find out. "I went to the Wonderland house because the opportunity presented itself and I know that when someone asks me if I want to see something, I just say yes without even thinking—because you'll regret it later on if you don't, that I've come to learn. So knowing it would be a rare opportunity to see such a notorious place first hand, I accepted the invitation."

Scott didn't have any particular interest in the house to begin with, but did say, "It's one of those LA stories that I know about, but never really studied. And I know that when the film came out, it didn't really strike a chord with me. The John Holmes connection was the most interesting thing to me, well, because of him, but I wasn't really interested until I got into the house. And that's when I became fascinated with it."

Scott is not particularly sensitive to the paranormal world, so I was curious to find out whether or not he "felt" anything when he went into the house.

"Well, my first impression was surprise because the house itself was so tiny. You walk outside and three feet in front of you is another house. I was expecting it to be this sprawling house and it is actually quite modest and the rooms are tiny. With all the windows that face out into the street, you feel like you are in a fishbowl.

"When we first walked in, the house just felt very quiet. And because I was there on sort of a research trip and spending a great deal of time holding up pictures of the crime scene, trying to match up where they happened, initially, no there wasn't a creepy feeling to the place.

"If I had been by myself, I probably would have been creeped out, but I was with a film crew, so when you are busy and have company, it makes all the difference in the world."

As Scott went from room to room trying to match up crime scene photos and the actual locations the bodies were found, he decided to recreate one of the actual police photos and placed himself in the location and the position of one of the victims. This is something he does every so often, he told me, explaining that he had actually sat on John Belushi's death bed and stood on the spot where Patsy Cline's body had been found, so it's kind of like, "So, I'm here…this is what I do now."

When Scott, who considers himself to be an open-minded skeptic, got home and uploaded his photos onto his computer, he was surprised to see that he had captured an orb in that one particular photo.

"When I first noticed the anomaly in the photo, I laughed and thought about you," he told me. "But that

Scott Michaels laying in the same place and position as one of the murder victims. Could the orb on the right actually be that victim in spirit?

was the weirdest but because when I was sitting up in that room where that body was found, and laying in that place, it was sort of like, 'Okay, I'm done here now. It wasn't like it was that creepy, but I got the urge to get out of there.

"I got up, and then Mike Dorsey, the director, did the same thing, and it wasn't until later on when I was going over the photographs that there it was; this was right at that particular moment that I was getting that feeling that it was time to leave, so that was kind of funny."

So with Scott not being particularly paranormally inclined, I wondered whether or not he thought the house on Wonderland might be haunted or perhaps should be, given the history of the place at the very least.

"Because of my experience with the Tate house, (referring to the infamous Manson murders) I think that because something so horrific happened here, with four people left for dead and one person who miraculously lived, and because it was such a horrible, violent crime, I don't think that the emotion was as strong in this house as it was in the Tate house. Those people were actually pleading for their lives—there was wildness going on—so I think for the most part, the victims in this crime were laying in bed and didn't know what hit them, therefore I don't necessarily think that that sort of raw emotion is hanging around. But I like to think that there is some sort of residue that people leave behind.

"I would have thought that because five people were beaten in that little tiny area that something's got to be around in there, but I was disappointed that nothing of a paranormal nature happened to us when we were there. And I shouldn't say this because one of these days something terrible will happen, but in the meantime, I could probably say with moderate confidence that there was something going on in there that made me feel weird."

At that point, the $64,000 question needed to be asked:

"Okay, Scott, if someone walked up to you right now, handed you the keys to the Wonderland house and told you it was all yours, would you live there?"

"Yeah, I probably would, not just because it is a murder house, but because it's in Laurel Canyon. It's a place that I love, and I love the Laurel Canyon vibe."

Knowing Scott as I do, is he inferring that Laurel Canyon vibes and murder vibes are one in the same? I'm inclined to think so.

Bentley

Bentley the bird who sees spirits and wants them out!

It's no secret that I live in a haunted house, but up until recently it was only us humans who seemed to notice. We've seen full-blown apparitions, shadows darting from one room to another, belongings disappear only to be found in unusual places, and we often hear voices calling our names.

Three psychics have been here to confirm the goings on. Mark Nelson identified an older woman who seems

to like hanging out in the bathroom, Michael J. Kouri was inundated with spirits when he came to visit, and at one point, Victoria Gross felt as though many of the spirits who come in and out of this house are coming through a portal in the front bedroom. Not only did she do a clearing of the room, she also tried to close the portal, because leaving it open only invited strangers in.

For the most part, those spirits in visitation and the few that seem to be here all the time have not affected our pets in any way. It's always been my thought that the spirits were here long before the animals arrived, and our pets have always viewed them as "those other guys who live here." It's pretty obvious by their actions that Pipsqueak the cat and Kalli the dog see them all the time, but Bentley, our elderly cockatiel has never really given any indication that he either sees anything or, if he does, even cares...until quite recently.

Bentley has been with me for nearly twenty-five years. He and I have been through thick and thin and he's always been my little buddy. He's a true character who thinks very highly of himself and can often be found walking back and forth in front of the mirror wolf whistling at beautiful bird he sees there. Several times during the day, he breaks into song and serenades us with Yankee Doodle, Beethoven's Fifth symphony, and several other ditties of his own creation. He prefers whistling to talking, but he does say "Hello" first thing in the morning when I uncover his cage or when encountering a guest.

As he gets older, Bentley, like many senior citizens, has gotten a bit crotchety. He's old, by cockatiel standards, so I don't let his moods bother me too much,

except when he takes his frustrations out on me by flying onto my head and pecking at me like a woodpecker or landing on my shoulder only to give my earlobe a pretty hard nip.

At night, I cover his cage and he's content until morning, but in recent weeks, it seems as though Bentley has become afraid of the dark.

As soon as his cage is covered, he begins pecking at his chest and wings accompanied by a nervous chirp. A couple of times, he's pecked so hard that he knocked himself off balance and fell off his perch, and this behaviour was starting to worry me. I really thought that perhaps he was ill, or maybe getting a bit senile, but once he was uncovered and the light in the room was turned back on, he was fine again. Then I began hearing him say *hello* every so often when nobody was around.

After a couple of weeks of this strange behavior, I mentioned it to Dinah Roseberry, my editor and friend at Schiffer Books. She had told me that she was doing animal communication, which I found fascinating.

"What can I say?" said Dinah, "I've loved animals forever. More than people, in many cases!"

She then went on to explain how she got involved in this Dr. Doolittle-esqe pursuit.

"This was an amazing blessing in direct correlation to my work as a ghost hunter for the Chester County Paranormal Research Society and an author of ghost books and the paranormal. For the past two years, I have been under a rather sharp ghost-learning curve as I've been involved in one investigation after another and have become acquainted with varied ghost professionals including other hunters, psychics, witches, spiritualists, and science-oriented folks who've taught me an immeasurable amount about the world "on the other side." The first ghost I *saw* was at Elaine's Haunted Mansion in Cape May, New Jersey, as I was writing my book, *Cape May Haunts*. It was a cat! I was incredibly intrigued by this and wanted to know more about the animals in the world beyond. That interest was pushed nearly beyond my sanity threshold when my own dear dog died after living seventeen wonderful years with me. I was searching for the same answers as many who had gone down this path before me. As I was working on my Lancaster, Pennsylvania, ghost book, I was directed to an event at Longs Park for the nonprofit organization United Against Puppy Mills, where I met two wonderful animal communicators. They changed my life by reaching out to my dog on the other side. It was then that I knew that I wanted to do this wonderful thing for others.

"I'd already decided that there was to be an animal section for the book I was writing because of the varied stories and 'coincidences' (which I don't believe in) surrounding my research. So I went to a conference/ workshop on the topic, and not only learned about contacting animals on the other side, but also how to talk with living animals.

"It was a calling—a strong one—and I found that I loved talking to creatures who made the world a better place as much as I liked writing about ...well, the things I write about."

With that in mind, I asked her if there was any way she could do a reading on Bentley to see if he was okay and to check in with Pipsqueak and Kalli as well to see what might be going on.

First Session

Marla, I have a lemur and a leopard as my animal communicator guides and the lemur said, "I'm not doin'this one." He jumped off the leopard's back.

The leopard said, "He said the bird was crotchety."

"I don't care, I'm not doin it," said the lemur and moved away.

The leopard looks up at me and strolls on, with me following, "The bird's already here," he said.

The bird I saw looked immediately like the bird on the old television show with that actor who was up for murder—I forget right now the name of the show. You know who I mean? The cop show! [Oh, as I'm rereading this for errors, it came to me: Baretta.] And I can't remember what you said your bird was, so I'm not sure if that's right or not. Then I realized there was more to that. He was like that bird in personality. I said to him:

"Hi, I'm--" and he immediately broke me off.

"Go to hell. I'm not talkin to you," he said.

Startled, I said, "but I wanted to talk to you for Marla—your mom—"

"Go to hell, I got nothin to say to you. You don't know nothin."

"I don't disagree," I said. But then I got the feeling again about the TV bird and knew that this bird thought he was a private detective of sorts and that he had major importance in his household. In charge. No nonsense. The boss. Nose in everything. For the sake of the many.

I said, "Just give me a message for her."

"Tell her to fix the damn perch."

I said, "What's wrong with your perch?"

"It hurts my feet."

"Is it broken?"

"No, it's old and worn. Don't I deserve to have a new one?"
(This was said ....well crotchety like and not in a nice polite way.)

"I'll tell her."

"Go to hell, I got nothing to say. I'm not talkin to you anymore."

And he was gone....

When I read that Bentley had told Dinah to *go to hell*, it sounded so much like him, I couldn't help but laugh, but I was pretty sure that there was more to what he was feeling then complaining about his perch, so I asked her once again to try and find out what it was about the dark that was frightening him.

Her reply was as follows:

I asked why he was chewing himself and I saw a shadow. It was a billowing kind of thing. I said to you, there seems to be a shadow in the room? You said where? I asked Bently and he said in the corner. Then I saw it hovering in the corner in my mind—it filled the corner and had dark blacks, grays, and whites in it. It was an empty corner. It was human height but did not reach the floor as I recall. Bentley was not actually afraid of it, rather disturbed that it was in his space. It made him uncomfortable and he wanted it to go away. He was nervous about it.

When Dinah told me about the shadow in the corner of the room, it really creeped me out because just a couple of days before, Ken came in from outside, walked into my office and said, "I don't think you're going to like what

I'm going to say, but when I walked in the front door, I saw a huge shadowy figure dart into the bedroom (which is adjacent to my office). It was really big, and definitely male. I saw him more clearly than any of the other spirits that I've seen in here."

And it was that night that Bentley began pecking at himself when the lights were turned off.

The most obvious solution to me was to leave Bentley's cage uncovered at night and leave a light on for him and that seemed to work, but I really wanted to solve the problem completely and make sure that this was really what was going on, so I asked Dinah if she could try and "talk" to Pipsqueak and Kalli to see what they had to say, because while Kalli still seemed oblivious to it all, Pipsqueak, who usually spent her days in the bedroom sleeping on the bed, suddenly decided to move into my office and hang out under my desk instead.

Second Session

Marla, I talked briefly this morning with Pipsqueak. She's fine and says that she sees shadows and such all the time, but they are no big deal. The caution is that Bentley is noticing something when he normally doesn't care. She thinks this warrants attention and thinks that sticking close to you (under the desk) as she watches is a best bet. She says that Bentley usually has a good take on things and if he's nervous, maybe she should think about it more. (Did Bentley poop on something of hers?)

Kalli can't be bothered with this shadow nonsense, but will allow Pip to check it out just in case. Kalli thinks the bird has issues.

After Ken heard what the critters had to say, he wondered if we shouldn't try and to do something to make this shadow person leave. Strangely enough, I didn't feel that he was malevolent in any way, but I did call on my guides to escort him away. That night, I was able to cover Bentley's cage and he slept well, but the reprieve was short-lived.

Next (From Dinah)

I had my guides take me to Bentley again. This time the lemur sat on the leopard and both animals stood to the rear at one side of me as I called out to Bentley. "Bentley, I know you don't like talking to me, but you are so beautiful and you're pecking yourself again. Marla is worried about you."

He's not as mean as before. "I know, I know."

"What's going on?"

"You already know. It's the shadow. It's still here."

"But I told you that you were protected by Marla."

"Yes, but it's still here and it smirks at me. I don't like that. It needs to go away."

"Do you understand that sometimes, it's not that easy to make something go when we don't understand it?

"What's to understand? It's a shadow. Make it go."

"Do you know how to make it go?"

"You people are supposed to know how to do that."

"It's not that easy, but I do tell you that you are protected and that you shouldn't let it annoy you or pay any attention to it smirking."

"Easy for you to say. Look, just make it go away."

"Do you want Marla to move your cage?"

"What, hey, am I talkin' to myself here? Make the shadow go away. Not me."

He says: *"The big furball knows how to make it go."*

"You mean Kalli?"

"It doesn't like their kind. The one is trying, but both of 'em need to chase it out. That other one doesn't care about me."

"Are you saying that cats should hang out where the shadow has been seen? And that it doesn't like them?"

"It doesn't care for me either, but I don't bother it. It smirks— even when I talk to it. I know I shouldn't but how else will she know it's around at other times?"

"She has trouble sleeping with the light on and is worried about you pecking your pretty self."

"Then…get…rid…of…the…thing. Nothing was done to get rid of it."

"Do you know who it is?"

[[The name Paul jumped into my head—haven't got a clue—it didn't come from Bentley, was just there]]

To Bentley, "Do you know who it is?"

[Now into my head: It's one of the Beatles. Marla, I'm going nuts I think. LOL]

"Is that you Bentley? Talking to me?"

"I got nothing to say, I told you that before. Just make it go."

Get the furballs on Bentley's reference to the "cats" kind of took me by surprise because there is only one cat in residence, but there once were four. Old age and infirmity took the other three over the past few years. Could Bentley have seen a cat spirit as well and not known the difference between the living and the dead?

I asked Dinah to tell Bentley that not only would I talk to Pipsqueak about trying to get the shadow person out, but that I would also try and banish him myself.

Note from Dinah

I tried talking to Bentley to tell him what you were going to do, and to let him know that I was confused over the cat/dog/Beatle thing and he just said:

"Give it a rest." (in characteristic tone).

It seems as though my best intentions didn't pan out, because that night Bentley was back to pecking when I turned out the lights and so back on they went.

I had asked Dinah earlier that day if she could ask Bentley what that "other" cat he saw looked like, and the next morning she sent me an email with the description Bentley gave her and it didn't match any of our previous cats. Strange.

Since the entity had still not gone, I called up my friend psychic Lisa J. Smith just to see if she perhaps knew who the intruder in the house might be, and she immediately said that our uninvited guest was a man named Frank.

At first, that didn't ring any bells, but a few days later, I was guesting on the NorCal Ghost Talk radio show and was retelling the story about the hitchhiking spirit we picked up at the Hollywood Bank building we investigated several months before (the story of that investigation can be found in *Ghosts of Hollywood 2: Talking to Spirits*) and then it dawned on me that his name was Frank as well. So it seems that even though I asked "Frank" at the time to go back to the bank, it appears that he's still around.

As of this writing, Bentley is still afraid of the dark and we're still sleeping with the lights on, Dinah continues to try and calm his ruffled feathers, and I'm still working on getting Frank to leave.

Ghost Hunting at the Hollywood Roosevelt Hotel

From our balcony in haunted Cabana Room 213.

J ust when you think you've reached the end of a book, an opportunity to do a little bit of ghost hunting presents itself and cannot be put off until later. Such was the case when I got a call from my friend, Scott Michaels, telling me the tale of a grisly ghost that supposedly haunts one of the poolside cabana rooms at the Hollywood Roosevelt Hotel. What he told me gave mc chills.

There have been many hauntings reported at the Hollywood Roosevelt over the years but this one was something new.

The Hollywood Roosevelt was named after president Theodore Roosevelt and opened in a gala ceremony on May 15, 1927, by its owners Douglas Fairbanks, his wife, Mary Pickford, and movie mogul Louis B. Meyer. The luxury hotel was designed to serve the new movie industry, and in keeping with that theme, the first Academy Award ceremony was held in the hotel's Blossom Room in 1929. The motion picture Academy held their meetings there from 1927 to 1935.

Over the years, the Roosevelt has continued to host the most prestigious movie stars of the day. In 1984, and again in 2005, the hotel underwent extensive restorations and since then, the Roosevelt ghosts have been putting in frequent appearances.

One of the most common paranormal occurrences happens at the front desk on a regular basis. Ghostly guests have been known to ring the switchboard from rooms that have since been remodeled and no longer exist.

In the Blossom Room, it's been reported that a little girl spirit called Caroline is said to be searching for her mother, and the figure of a very agitated man is often seen walking back and forth, as if on a mission. There is also a cold spot at one end of the room that never goes away. Some paranormal researchers believe that it is a portal to the other side where spirits come in and out at will.

Actor Montgomery Clift stayed in Room 928 during the making of *From Here to Eternity* and rumor has it you can still hear him practicing his bugle in the hall that leads to that room. Many unknowing guests staying in Room 928 have called downstairs to the front desk in the middle of the night to complain about the racket.

Early in her modeling career, Marilyn Monroe lived in one of the cabanas next to the swimming pool which

contained a beautiful full-length mirror. The mirror is now hanging in the main building where some say they still see her image gazing back at them. Monroe also posed on the diving board of the hotel's swimming pool for her first print ad and there are many reports of seeing her ghost on a lounge chair near the pool reenacting that photo shoot.

It appears that the third-floor penthouse suite, where Clark Gable and Carole Lombard once secretly trysted before going public with their love, seems to hold a place in the hearts of these ill-fated lovebirds because there are frequent reports that their ghosts come back every so often to relive those tender moments. But there is nothing tender about the ghost that haunts Cabana Room 213.

My regular team members, Barry Conrad, psychic Victoria Gross and Scott Michaels, were excited about the investigation when I told them about it

**Barbara Nelson, Mark Nelson, Victoria Gross and Barry Conrad
arriving at the Roosevelt.**

and immediately said they'd be there. And since the investigation appeared to have a lot of potential, I also asked psychic Mark Nelson and his wife, Barbara, to join us as well as Psychic to the Stars, Kenny Kingston, who is quite familiar with the hotel and its resident ghosts, and his associate, Valerie Porter. This was a case of "the more psychics the better" in my opinion and I was anxious to hear the impressions that each of them would have.

Since the room was booked for twenty-four hours, and none of the investigation team would be able to stay overnight except for me, I called upon my good friend, Virginia Fegley, to come along as well, not only because she herself is quite psychic, but also because I needed a partner in crime to stay with me in the wee hours after everyone else had left.

Scott had told us that because the hotel was keeping this haunting quite hush-hush, it would be better not to say anything to the front desk person who checked us in about our reason for being there, but the minute I told the clerk that we were checking into Room 213, his facial expression and raised eyebrows gave him away.

"Is there anything wrong?" I asked.

"No, that's a very nice room," he replied, looking rather uncomfortable and a bit self conscious.

"Then why the strange expression?" I wondered.

At that point, he just kind of smiled and shrugged.

Because he looked as though he was ready to explode, I took my index finger and mimed slashing my throat to see if that would illicit a response because that is how the ghost of Room 213 presents himself.

"YOU KNOW!" he exclaimed, and then I went on to admit the reason we were checking in. "How did

Virginia Fegley on the balcony preparing for the night ahead.

you find out about it?" he asked. "I thought only hotel employees knew."

Without naming names, I explained that it was a hotel employee who spilled the beans.

Since we checked in early and the room wasn't ready, Ginny and I decided to go wait by the pool. Michael Caputo, the man at the front desk joined us a few minutes later and told us his version of the story about the grisly sighting.

"One of the hotel employees went into the room to see if it needed cleaning, and saw that housekeeping had already been there. This was about three o'clock in the afternoon. As she was leaving the room, she turned back and saw a man that was solid hovering above the bed. He had no feet, he had a slit in his throat, his face was blue and black, and he had blood all over his clothes. He just stared at her and at that point she ran out of the room, and we have her on security camera as soon as she left the room and then fainting in the hallway.

"There was also one man who came to the front desk late at night, and just said that the room needs to be condemned. We asked him what happened, and he said that there was something wrong with the mirrors in the room, it should be condemned, and that's all he told us.

"The ghost being sighted happened about four months ago, and by the way, our co-worker who saw the ghost doesn't work here anymore, and the man who said the room needs to be condemned was about a month after that. And keep in mind they've been doing a lot of construction around here, redoing a lot of the old cabanas, and lots of things like this happen when there is construction going on."

By the time Ginny and I checked into the room, the ghost stories had started to take their toll because as soon as we got inside, Ginny set down her suitcase and purse right beside the front door. I mentioned that it might look better if she stashed them in the bedroom before our guests got there, but her reply was, "But what if we need to run out of here in a hurry? At least we'll be able to grab our stuff on the way out." I couldn't argue with logic, so there it stayed.

We had an hour or so to kill before our guests were scheduled to arrive, so we decided to walk through the suite and get our impressions and then call room service for a quick bite.

There was a definite heaviness to the place, and even though the room was bright and sunny, it just felt plain "cold." We weren't picking up on anything in particular except for the fact that the suite was anything but welcoming, but when we walked into the bathroom we changed our minds.

The layout of the bathroom was strange. Just to the left of the bedroom was a small dressing room area, and also a door leading into to the bathroom. When I opened the door, I saw that the room was quite long and narrow. The sink and vanity were on the left side and the shower just opposite. Down at the far end of the room was a divider wall and the toilet sat on the other side of it.

The shower curtain was drawn and as we walked past it, I felt like someone behind the curtain was going to jump

The "dreaded" bathroom that we all tried to avoid.

out and grab me. By the time Ginny and I reached the far end of the room, we had both decided that it felt so creepy in there that if either of us needed to use the bathroom throughout the night—which we undoubtedly would—we would have to use the Buddy System, because neither of us wanted to go back in there alone.

We had our dinner out on the balcony overlooking the pool and it wasn't too long before Psychic to the Stars Kenny Kingston arrived with his associate Valerie Porter and his goddaughter. While we sat in the living room waiting for the others, Kenny mentioned offhandedly that there was a spirit of a man in the bedroom who seemed to be undressing.

After a few minutes, Kenny and Valerie did a walk around, and they both agreed that there was something unpleasant about the entire suite. Valerie in particular

Valerie, Kenny, Missy, and Barry Conrad talking about the very haunted room.

Kenny Kingston investigating the bathroom at the Roosevelt.

mentioned that she got the impression of blood smeared on the bathroom walls from the shower to the toilet and all the way down the walls. She also said that the bathroom seemed rather "tomb-like." This was an interesting choice of words because all of the psychics who were there that night used the same words to describe the bathroom independent of each other. Valerie also mentioned hearing a woman crying and the words, "It didn't have to happen."

It was Kenny's thought that numerology-wise, Room 213 equaled the number 6 and that should have made the suite a perfect home, but he said, "The people who were involved in the renovation of this room have contributed to the problem. They brought in negative spirits and left them here. People here were damned."

Scott Michaels was the next to arrive, then came Meredith McDonald, the hotel employee who tipped us off about the room in the first place, and then Mark Nelson and his wife, Barbara.

As Mark was walking through the suite, he felt a great deal of chaos in the bedroom. "I feel violence and turmoil," he said. "There's quite a bit of heaviness in the air as well."

Scott was quick to agree. "I'm feeling that too," he said, "and it's weird because I don't usually get that kind of thing."

Mark also got the impression that the spirit in the room, most likely the one who appeared to the hotel employee, was sort of "hanging back" lurking about, and almost smirking at us all. As he was saying that, Ginny snapped a photo of him and the picture clearly shows a black shadow against the curtains all the way to the left of the photo that looks nothing like the shadow Mark would have cast.

When I sent the photo to Scott the next day, his reply was, "Interesting, that's the creepy corner I had a problem with. Chest heavy, very freaky."

Our next stop was the bathroom, and Mark immediately got the impression of a woman being stabbed to death. "It was a crime of passion and took place sometime in the 1950s," he said. "She had been here for a couple of days with her boyfriend, and then things went bad. This was not a premeditated murder, but the man did have blood on his hands, meaning that he was a violent type to begin with and had killed before. I feel like this woman is trapped here and while he isn't trapped, he comes back in visitation often because he knows that she is still here."

Mark also mentioned that he thought this particular spirit was the type to make his presence known in a

Mark Nelson and the shadow on the wall.
Was this our ghastly ghost making his presence known?

violent fashion. "He is the type who will throw things in here, slam doors, and knock things off the vanity. He likes to scare people, so don't be surprised if things in this room get noisy tonight after everyone else has gone."

That statement was not music to my ears, and only made the thought of Ginny and I alone in the room even more foreboding.

While we were waiting for Victoria Gross and Barry Conrad to arrive, I was in the bedroom on the phone when I noticed Meredith come into the room. It looked as though she was pulling tiny bits of paper out of her hand and studying them. When I got off the phone, she explained that she was in fact, a Druid Priest, and that she was pulling runes, to get the feel for each room.

"When I went into the bathroom," she told me, "the rune that came up was the worst possible one you can get."

Why wasn't I surprised?

When Victoria and Barry arrived, Victoria walked through the suite while Barry set up the camera for the séance. Her impressions matched the other psychic's exactly, and she commented that she felt an "ugly, hairy guy in the bathroom who had a low intelligence base" and was perhaps a bit mentally slow.

It seemed to me that there were more spirits in the room than we expected.

At about 9 pm, we all gathered around the large coffee table in the living room and began the séance.

Barry Conrad, Kenny Kingston and Victoria Gross thinking happy thoughts before our séance began.

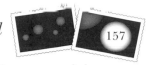

I was secretly hoping that the grisly apparition would come and let the mediums cross him over so that Ginny and I would have a worry-free night, but that wasn't the case.

In a séance, you never know who is going to come through, and between Kenny, Mark, and Victoria, we all got messages from loved ones, and at one point, Scott and a few others noticed that the table began to vibrate and jiggle a bit which was strange for two reasons. One, that table was so heavy it could not be moved, and secondly, not one of us was touching the table when that happened.

At one point, Valerie said she "saw" syringes and razor blades on the table and Mark picked up on the spirit of a man who he said died of a heroin overdose in that room.

Mark was taping the séance, and when he reviewed the tape the next day, there was, what sounded like an EVP of a deep sigh when Mark mentioned the poor soul's name who overdosed.

He also picked up on the spirit of the woman who he saw being killed in the bathroom. He said that she wanted to cross over, and he assisted her in doing so. The man who died of the overdose seemed to want to cross, but we don't think he actually went.

Not long after that, Valerie, who was sitting to my left, asked me if I felt a coldness between us, and I admitted that I did. She smiled and said there was a large reddish dog, in spirit, sitting between us. A few minutes later, I felt the coldness move over a bit and something definitely brushed my hand. Hopefully, it was the wagging of a happy dog spirit's tail.

Shortly thereafter, Kenny seemed to go into a deep trance and began to mumble. A second later, he began

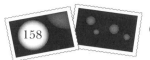

speaking, but the voice that came out of his mouth was that of an old woman. She told us that her name was Elizabeth and we all welcomed her in. Then she explained that she used to live at the hotel and is there all the time. She said she didn't like all the renovation that was taking place and said that the hotel was filled with "nuts" these days and that wasn't the case in her day. She went on to say that her last name was Patterson and that she hoped we had seen some of her movies.

The name Elizabeth Patterson was familiar to me, although I couldn't place it, but Scott recognized her right away and told us that Ms. Patterson was the actress who played the part of Mrs. Trumble in the old *I Love Lucy* series, and that she did, in fact, live at the Roosevelt way back when.

Throughout the course of the séance, spirits came and went, and then after about an hour, it was time to close the circle. I was disappointed that our grisly ghost did not make an appearance.

Victoria had brought some nibbles for us all and food is a great way to ground yourself after talking to spirits, so we all sat around, ate, and talked, and then one by one, the group began to diminish in size as people began to leave.

After everyone had gone, Ginny and I picked up the living room and then went out on the balcony. It was about 2 am and the bar across the way was closing. For the first time that night, things were very quiet. Too quiet, in fact, so we went back in and turned on the television for a little bit of noise.

A few minutes later, Victoria called us from the car saying that they ran into a hotel employee on their way out and asked him if the hotel was indeed haunted. He

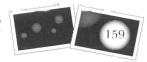
said that the two most haunted spots were The Blossom Room and Room 213. He also mentioned that there were only two maids working in the entire hotel who would go in and clean in our room.

Ginny and I decided early in the evening that besides using the bathroom together, that we weren't going to get undressed or go into the bedroom to try and get some sleep. In fact, it was decided that we weren't going to sleep at all because Mark had mentioned that this particular spirit was the type to sneak up and appear to people who's defenses were down. And neither of us wanted to wake up with a grisly apparition hovering above us.

Because it was so quiet, I thought it might be a good time to try and get some EVP, but whether it was our imaginations gone wild or a really creepy feel in the room, neither of us wanted to walk into the bedroom or

The bedroom where a grisly ghost appeared to a hotel employee.

the bathroom. The best we could do was to dash over to the hallway with the camcorder and point it towards the bedroom and leave it there for a few minutes, then move it into the bathroom for a while. EVP, we decided, would have to wait until the light of day when, we hoped, the atmosphere would "lighten up" as well. Meanwhile, we spent our time talking both in the living room and outside on the balcony. At one point, Ginny shot three photos in succession off the balcony but in the second photo this weird mist appeared that was not in the first or the third picture.

Time may fly when you're having fun, but the hours between 3-6 am dragged on and on. We were too scared to move about, truly bored, and feeling rather sleep-deprived resulting in several episodes of the uncontrollable giggles.

Strange mist—the second of three pictures taken, one right after the other, revealed this odd anomoly.

But at first light, we were able to get up off the couch and do our EVP work. We gathered our stuff together, left everything right by the door, and proceeded to try and talk to spirit. Ginny was taking pictures with her camera throughout the session and, coincidentally or not, the more I urged whoever might be around to talk to us, the more orbs kept showing up in her photos.

We left the hotel quite bleary-eyed shortly after that and, as we were leaving the building, Ginny turned around and snapped a picture of the hallway, which, also coincidentally, was filled with orbs. Could that have been an ethereal goodbye from the ghosts of the Hollywood Roosevelt?

In the days following our investigation, I asked the psychics who were there to sum up their impressions or investigation and here is what they had to say:

Kenny Kingston

"I'm not a psychic/medium who dwells on negativity, so I don't automatically look for it when I enter a location. But I do feel some unhappy events took place in the room. When my companion and writer Valerie Porter and I entered the room we said simultaneously "Johns." I identified a spirit with that name but also sensed Johns as associated with prostitution. I also feel serious drug deals happened there.

"However, if guests have complained about unusual activity in the room, I feel it's because they don't understand the spirit world. I didn't feel negative or harmful spirits in the room. They wanted to be recognized and blessed and I feel we gave them that opportunity. Also, the new décor is (according to the spirits who spoke to me) "coldly modern" and they're unhappy with it and want their opinions known.

Downstairs orbs.
As we were leaving, Ginny turned and took this photo in the empty hallway.

"It's only natural when I began the séance that I also brought in spirits and messages meant for those attending the séance—you can't censor psychic information and it was flowing freely that evening. Is the room totally "cleansed?" I doubt it. I would want to bring a Bible, Holy water, and salt to do a complete cleansing. There are too many vibrations in a hotel the age of the Roosevelt to expect to remove them in one session. Not every spirit has yet to be identified."

Victoria Gross

"When I walked into the bathroom, I sensed a very large man throwing things around. He was a brutal man with low intelligence. He was very hairy—dark hair.

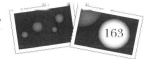

The bedroom felt very violent to me. I felt the same man throwing a woman around. I was drawn to the northeast corner and when I stood in the corner I felt a cold spot—chills ran through my body. It felt as if my back was being pushed up against the wall and I was trapped.

During the séance, I sensed a woman in a long white satin nightgown (or gown) that was watching us from the bedroom door. She was from the thirties or forties. Her spirit was very gentle. She was not the woman that was beaten by the man—that was a different time period. That woman had black short hair.

Mark Nelson

When I first walked into Room 213 at the Hollywood Roosevelt, I was immediately hit by a sense of violent death and assault. Specifically, I felt as if someone had been killed with a knife, with multiple and brutal slashes. It had been a crime of passion, because it felt like a real mess. Specifically, the bathroom felt like a tomb. I believe that the death occurred in that room. I also believe three spirits were still in that room. They included the murderer (who also died a violent death), his female victim, and another male energy who died of an overdose in or near the room. I also believe the murderer was killed violently, in retribution for killing the woman. I felt the murderer was staying back and watching us that night. We would have been tougher to scare, because we were expecting him. I also feel the female energy might appear in the bathroom, specifically in the mirror. Other than that, it was a perfectly nice room.

Mark Nelson and Victoria Gross before the séance.

The living room, when Ginny and I arrived.

**Mark Nelson, Kenny Kingston and Barbara Nelson
—a meeting of the psychic minds.**

Kenny Kingston and Meredith McDonald. Two great minds thinking alike.

Barbara Nelson and Scott Michaels.
Looks like Barbara is pondering the orb over Scott's head.

Mark Nelson and Scott Michaels talking things over during the investigation.

The view from the balcony at the Roosevelt.

The Ambassador Hotel
3400 Wilshire Boulevard

The Ambassador Hotel shortly before it was torn down.

The famed Ambassador Hotel opened its doors on New Year's Day 1921. The hotel boasted 500 rooms and sat on 23.7 acres on Wilshire Boulevard.

The Ambassador's site was originally a part of Reuben Schmidt's dairy farm until 1902. That year, Schmidt sold a twenty-three-acre section to Ella Crowell. She then sold half of the land to the Los Angeles Pacific Railway Company for the purpose of constructing an interurban railway. The railway plans did not materialize, and in 1919, both Mrs. Crowell and the railway company sold their halves to the hotel company.

In June 1919, ground was broken and construction started on the estimated $5 million hotel. The Los

Angeles and Wilshire area Chambers of Commerce devised the idea of a hotel as a civic endeavor. In 1919, the Wilshire area was considered to be too far from developed areas to have much value. In addition, it was believed that Los Angeles would develop in an eastward movement, instead of towards the sea. The placement of the Ambassador was the major impetus behind the development of Wilshire Boulevard into one of L.A.'s main arteries. The hotel was originally called "The California," however, its name was changed to the "Ambassador," after a man named S.W. Straus stepped in with much-needed construction funding. The hotel then became a part of the Ambassador Hotels chain, which included hotels in Atlantic City, New York, Santa Barbara, and The Alexandria in Los Angeles.

The hotel would go on to serve as the stomping grounds for a staggering list of Hollywood legends, heads of state, and an endless list of famous personalities from the Twentieth Century. Presidents Hoover, Roosevelt, Truman, Eisenhower, Kennedy, Johnson, and Nixon stayed there. When Soviet Leader Nikita Khrushchev visited the U.S. in 1959, he stayed at the Ambassador. Marilyn Monroe had her start here as a model, as a client of a poolside modeling agency. Howard Hughes and Jean Harlow were some of the many longtime residents who made it their home for a time.

For decades, the hotel's famed Cocoanut Grove was *the* hot spot for live entertainment on the West Coast, where people like Bing Crosby and Barbra Streisand had their start, and Frank Sinatra, Sammy Davis Jr., and many others came to perform. Gene Kelly, Diana Ross, Judy Garland, Louis Armstrong, Nat "King" Cole, and Julie Andrews all played the Grove.

In later years, The Ambassador is probably best known as the place where Robert Kennedy was assassinated after winning the California Primary in 1968. Ironically, the hotel was featured in the 2006 film "Bobby," which tells the story about that fateful night. This was the last time The Ambassador was used as a movie location.

The hotel officially closed to the public in 1989. Since that time, the fate of the Hotel changed hands many times. In 1989, Donald Trump purchased the site for $64 million with plans to develop a high-rise hotel, but withdrew from the project shortly thereafter. In 1990, Ambassador Films was established. It was a private company renting the hotel out for film production. Then, in December 2001, the Los Angeles Unified School District won development rights to the hotel. Their efforts were thwarted in April 2004 when demolition was suspended due to a lawsuit with Los Angeles Conservancy who fought tooth and nail to keep the hotel intact. Unfortunately, they lost the fight and in 2005 demolition began.

As of this writing, three new schools are to be built on the site of the Ambassador: an elementary school, scheduled to open in 2008, a middle school and a high school, scheduled to open in 2009, but one can't help but wonder whether or not the children attending these schools will be spending time in class with some other-worldly classmates.

Before the hotel was demolished, witnesses reported seeing a ghostly figure in a window on the hotel's fourth floor, only to lean out and disappear. Lights were seen turning on and off by themselves, lights were seen streaking down the hallways, and many people claimed that the Ambassador was riddled with cold spots.

Haunted... Or Not Haunted?

S ometimes we run across a location that clearly should have their fair share of spirit activity, but the owners of the property don't want any sort of investigation and are not forthcoming with any information that would validate our suspicions.

There are a great many places in Hollywood that fall into this category and I decided to turn my "No, You Cannot Investigate Here" list into a "I Hope They Change Their Mind" list and in the meantime, thought I'd share these locations with you. Perhaps you've visited one of these places and have a story or two to pass on to me.

Barney's Beanery

T he world famous Barney's Beanery first opened in 1920 as a destination for westbound travelers on the old Route 66. Weary travelers could turn in their license plates in exchange for a free pint of beer. Then in 1927, John "Barney" Anthony took over the helm. Barney is said to have been a genial host who made all his customers feel right at home and also helped out the hungry masses when they had no money to pay for their meals. In fact, when new ownership took over several years ago, they unearthed a drawer full of I.O.U. slips from people who had been down on their luck. Clark Gable was one of them, along with several others who went on to become big Hollywood stars.

Serving up delicious food and big dollops of compassion for mankind, Barney's soon became a

Barney's Beanery—a Hollywood landmark restaurant.

favorite local hangout for studio folk, tourists, and the locals as well.

By the 1950s, it was a Mecca for beatniks and rock and rollers, and by the mid 1960s, Barney had become an epicenter for arts and culture and a favorite hangout for people like Jimi Hendrix and Jim Morrison (who was once tossed out of the place for urinating on the bar). Janis Joplin had her last drink there before going back to her room at the Landmark Hotel where she died later that night from a heroin overdose. The 1970s and 80s brought in the punk and new wave crowd, but with them came celebrities like Elliot Gould, Bette Midler, Liza Minelli, and Mel Gibson. More recently, Quentin Terantino wrote much of *Pulp Fiction* in his favorite booth by the bar, and a sad development in mid-September 2008, a man was fatally stabbed outside Barney's following an argument ocurring inside the restaurant.

These days, anyone who is anyone, and even those who aren't, are mingling together and enjoying Barney's wonderful atmosphere and mouth-watering food and spirits. In fact, the menu is so huge, it's not a good idea to come so hungry you're on the verge of passing out, because unless you're a regular and know what you want, it's going to take quite a while to get through it all.

When I spoke to General Manager A.J. Sacher on the phone, he said that in addition to all the lively folk who frequent Barney's Beanery these days, he suspects that there may very well be a few unseen customers who, it seems, keep coming back for more...from the afterlife. To date, no invitation to investigate has been forthcoming, but I remain forever hopeful.

Capitol Records Building

The thirteen-story Capitol Records Building at 1730 Vine Street building was built in 1956, reportedly at the urging of label artists Nat "King" Cole and Johnny Mercer.

The building is still the headquarters of Capitol Records and is also one of the most recognizable buildings in Hollywood. It is a myth that the round structure was designed to resemble a stack of records topped with a stylus, but the landmark building is unique in a number of other ways as well. Designed by noted architect Welton Becket, it is the world's first office building in the form of a round tower and the modern, striking, earthquake-resistant reinforced-concrete structure is 13 stories tall and

The Capitol Records Tower really does look like a stack of records.

150 feet high, the maximum building height permitted in Los Angeles at the time. A flashing beacon at the top of the building spells out "H-O-L-L-Y-W-O-O-D" to passing aircraft.

The building houses a recording studio renowned for its acoustics. Artists who have used it include Judy Garland, Nat "King" Cole and the Beach Boys. Studio A in this building was inaugurated on February 22, 1956, by Frank Sinatra, recording the instrumental album "Tone Poems of Color." Sinatra recorded many of his classic albums here in the 1950s.

The decor is in keeping with the outward appearance of the building. The ground floor, the only rectangular part of the building, is actually a separate structure which surrounds the tower and was joined to it after the entire tower was completed. It houses the Recording Department offices, tape-to-disk dubbing rooms, and three recording studios which were designed to be as modern and striking as the building itself.

Two music superstars have their "Walk of Fame" stars in front of the building: John Lennon and Garth Brooks.

The building was sold by its owner in 2006 for fifty million dollars, but there is no doubt in my mind that the spirits are still having impromptu recording sessions when nobody else is around.

The Playboy Mansion

Hugh Hefner's 22,000-square-foot house in Holmby Hills is described as being in the "Gothic-Tudor" style and sits on 5.3 acres. It was built by architect Arthur R. Kelly in 1927 and acquired by Playboy in 1971 for about $1.2 million. It sits close to the extreme northwestern corner of the exclusive Los Angeles Country Club, near UCLA and the Bel-Air Country Club. Over the years, approximately $15 million has been invested in renovating and expanding the mansion, and the current market value of the home is $50 million.

The mansion has 22 rooms including a wine cellar, a game room, a private zoo and aviary (and related pet cemetery), tennis courts, a waterfall, and a large swimming pool area (including a patio and barbecue area, the famous grotto, a sauna, and a bathhouse). These features and many others have been frequently showcased on television.

The game room, a separate building on the property's north-side, is more properly called a game

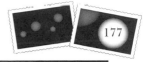

The Playboy Mansion—and no, that's not Hef's car.

house. From the fountain in front of the main entrance, there are two sidewalks, which run past a wishing-well. The sidewalk on the right leads to the game house and runs past a Hollywood Star of Hugh Hefner. Its front entrance opens to a game room with a pool table in the center. This room has a number of vintage and modern arcade games, pinball machines, player piano, jukebox, television, stereo, and couch. The game house has two wings. Walking to the left, one finds a room with a soft cushioned floor, mirrors all around, television, and an exit. There is also a restroom with a shower. The right wing of the game house has a smaller restroom, and entrance to a bedroom. This bedroom is also connected to another bedroom, which has an exit to the rear backyard of the game house. The game house has a backyard with lounge chairs, and gates on either side.

The home became famous during the 1970s because of Hefner's lavish parties. According to one of Hef's girlfriends, Bridget Marquardt, the Mansion is the only private residence in the city of Los Angeles with a permit for fireworks displays.

The residence next door is a mirror image of the Mansion layout, only smaller. Hefner purchased the neighboring building in 1996, and it is currently home to his separated wife Kimberley Conrad and their children. Hefner and Conrad married in 1989 and separated in 1998, although they have never divorced. Conrad said, in an E! True Hollywood Story episode, that she has no plans to get a divorce.

The original Playboy Mansion was a seventy-room residence in Chicago at 1340 North State Street. It was built in 1899 and acquired by Hefner in 1959. For a period in the 1970s, Hefner divided his time between the Chicago mansion and the Mansion West, moving fulltime to the California mansion in 1974. The Chicago mansion boasted a brass plate on the door with the Latin inscription, Si Non Oscillas, Noli Tintinnare ("If you don't swing, don't ring").

In 2002, Hefner purchased a house across the street from the Playboy Mansion specifically for the use of visiting Playmates.

My good friend, Psychic to the Stars Kenny Kingston and I were talking about the mansion not long ago. Kenny has been to the mansion and claims that there are two ghosts residing there, one of a man and another a woman.

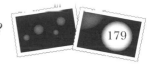
The Earl Carroll Theater
6230 Sunset Boulevard

The Earl Carroll Theater 2008

Impresario and showman Earl Carroll built two impressive theaters during his life. The first was on Broadway in New York at 753 Seventh Avenue and W. Fiftieth Street in New York City. Built in 1922, and highly successful for a number of years, it was eventually demolished and rebuilt on a much more lavish scale. It reopened in August of 1931 with Carroll's billing that it was "the largest legitimate theater in the world." However, the facility's operating costs proved astronomical and it went into foreclosure in early 1932, after which it was acquired by producer Florenz Ziegfeld who renamed it the "Casino Theatre."

Ziegfeld, too, went bankrupt only a short time later. The building was then converted to retail space in 1940 and eventually became a Woolworth's Department Store. It was demolished in 1990.

Earl Carroll built his second famous theater at 6230 Sunset Boulevard in Hollywood, California. It opened on December 26, 1938. As he had done at the New York theater, over the doors of the entrance, Carroll had emblazoned the words "Through these portals pass the most beautiful girls in the world."

As "entertainment palace," the glamorous supper club-theatre offered shows on a massive stage with a sixty-foot-wide double-revolving turntable and staircase, plus swings that could be lowered from the ceiling. The building's facade was adorned by what at the time was one of Hollywood's most famous landmarks: a twenty-foot-high neon head portrait of entertainer Beryl Wallace, one of Earl Carroll's "most beautiful girls in the world," who became his devoted companion.

The sign has long vanished, but a re-creation made from photos is today on display at Universal CityWalk, at Universal City, as part of the collection of historic neon signs from the Museum of Neon Art. Another major feature at the theater was its "Wall of Fame" where many of Hollywood's most glamorous stars inscribed a personal message.

The facility was a popular spot for many of Hollywood's most glamorous stars and powerful film industry moguls such as Darryl F. Zanuck and Walter Wanger who sat on the Earl Carroll Theatre's board of governors.

The theater was sold following the 1948 deaths of Earl Carroll and Beryl Wallace in the crash of United Airlines Flight 624 at Mount Carmel, Pennsylvania. The

theater continued to operate, but in the 1950s fell on hard times.

In 1953, the theater operated as a nightclub called "The Moulin Rouge" and had many incarnations after that, changing hands several times. It eventually became the "Hullabaloo Rock and Roll Club," capitalizing on the popularity of the 1960s television variety show *Hullabaloo*. It then became the "Aquarius Theater" in the late 1960s and was used as a venue for the long-running Rock musical "Hair" and made famous as the place where Jim Morrison and The Doors performed on July 21, 1969.

In 1983, the Pick-Vanoff Company purchased the property and converted it into a state-of-the art television theater that for nine years was the filming site of "Star Search." It later became the Nickelodeon Theater and was owned by Columbia Pictures. In 2004, the property was sold to a private equity firm as part of a larger parcel of property.

Whatever the building is destined to become, a new sign above the door should read, "Through These Portals, The Most Beautiful Girl Ghosts in the World."

The Hollywood Palladium
6215 Sunset Boulevard

For over a half century, the Hollywood Palladium has offered world-class entertainment—from legends of the Big Band era, to the best in contemporary rock concerts. Since opening it's doors, the nightclub/ballroom has consistently presented the highest caliber of music events possible, establishing itself as Hollywood's flagship for fun and excitement.

The Palladium began the vision of motion pictures producer/promoter Maurice M. Cohen—his personal dream to create the world's largest dining and dancing palace. Opened as a ballroom in 1940, the 11,000 square-foot oval dance floor was the place to be.

The Hollywood Palladium opened on October 29, 1940. The ballroom was designed with big band swing in mind and included, along with the fabulous acoustics, a spacious and beautiful solid white ash dance floor to accommodate the huge dance crowds. Chairs at tables provided seating for thousands, more in the balconies on both sides. Tommy Dorsey and his orchestra had the distinction of performing on opening night. Frank Sinatra, opened to rave reviews. Over 6,500 people attended each show, filling the dance floor, dining area, and mezzanine, and over the years, Glenn Miller, Stan Kenton, Les Brown, Artie Shaw, Harry James, and all the rest destined to become legends entertained the masses on the Palladium stage. It was truly the King of the ballrooms with enormous crowds throughout the Big Band era. Famed band leader Les Brown described those years at the Palladium as "New Year's Eve every night!"

In those days, the Palladium was situated between the NBC and CBS radio studios and dominated the night scene which included such celebrity haunts as the Brown Derby, Earl Carroll's and the Mocambo. Inside, familiar faces like Rita Hayworth, Tyrone Power, Lana Turner, and Betty Grable mingled with non-celebrity clientele who enjoyed the ballroom's entertainment and big band dancing at moderate prices.

As America entered World War II, the Palladium flourished and continued to provide the best in entertainment. For fifty cents, GIs spilling over from the nearby Hollywood Canteen could dance to top-named bands, and Stan Kenton's radio show brought the excitement of the Palladium into millions of homes nightly.

Even after the war, when big bands began to lose their popularity, the Palladium still drew in a record 6,750 eager dancers to the 1947 opening night performance of Tex Beneke and the Glenn Miller Orchestra—an event enthusiastically covered by *Life Magazine*.

The television came to the Palladium in the early fifties with a weekly one and one-half hour telecast over KNXT. In 1961, when two television producers became the new owners, they booked Lawrence Welk who drew an estimated 14,000 people for his first two nights. Over the next decade, the Hollywood Palladium became Welk's "home" for his popular weekly television broadcast.

As contemporary tastes have changed, so has the Hollywood Palladium's style of entertainment. The Rolling Stones, James Brown, Led Zeppelin, The Who, Rod Stewart, The Police, MTV's Lollapalooza Tour, Alice in Chains, Bon Jovi, and the Red Hot Chili Peppers have all performed in the landmark facility. The ballroom has even hosted such dignitaries as England's Princess Margaret and Lord Snowden, Robert Kennedy, Ronald Reagan, Adalai Stevenson, Harry S. Truman, Dwight D. Eisenhower, John F. Kennedy, Lyndon B. Johnson and Richard Nixon.

The Hollywood Palladium has been the site of many nationally televised events including the Emmy Awards, Grammy Awards, Entertainment Hall of Fame Awards,

Comedy Awards, NAACP Image Awards, Country Music Awards, and others. Location shooting has also been an important part of the facility's daily operation; and the Palladium has provided a backdrop for scenes including *The Bodyguard, What's Love Got to Do With It?, Mr. Saturday Night, 1941, The Sinatra Story* (mini-series) and the *"Blues Brothers."*

So is the Hollywood Palladium haunted? Do Lawrence Welk's champagne bubbles float amongst spectral dancers on a seemingly empty dance floor? Can the ghostly sound of screaming bobbysoxers be heard above Frank Sinatra's ethereal voice? I'd like to think so, and hopefully some day I'll be able to find out.

The Egyptian Theater
6712 Hollywood Boulevard

Charles E. Toberman, arguably the most important real estate developer in Hollywood in 1920, was looking for someone to bring a grand, first-class motion picture theater, like those prevalent in the downtown area, to Hollywood. Sid Grauman, who, within just a few short years in Los Angeles, after migrating from San Francisco, had built the deluxe, downtown Los Angeles movie palaces, the Million Dollar, the Rialto, and the Metropolitan, agreed to come to Hollywood after Toberman acquired the 6712 Hollywood Boulevard site, previously home of the thriving lemon ranch of an old lodge buddy. The buddy was willing to sell the property to Toberman because, between 1910 and 1920, the population of Hollywood increased from 5,000 to 36,000 and agriculture was practically abandoned, being

replaced by business and high-class residences, bungalow courts, and apartments.

Architects Meyer and Holler were hired to design the Egyptian Theater and the Milwaukee Building Company built it in eighteen months, at a cost of $800,000. Sid Grauman's final touches included building a 30 x 73 foot stage to accommodate the elaborate prologues that proceeded film presentations. The prologue prior to Cecil B. DeMille's *The Ten Commandments* featured over 100 costumed performers including "players seen in their identical roles in the flesh and blood." Each prologue was advertised as more incredible and spectacular than the last and it is said that Grauman oversaw every detail himself.

The first film to open at the Egyptian was *Robin Hood* starring Douglas Fairbanks. The Grand Opening premiere was on Wednesday, October 18, 1922. The film reportedly cost over one million dollars to make and Grauman selected the opera Aida as the overture.

Tickets were $5 for the premiere and audiences could reserve a seat up to two weeks in advance for the daily performances. Evening admission was $.75, $1, or $1.50. The film was not shown in any other Los Angeles theater that year.

At the dedication ceremonies, those who spoke congratulated Sid Grauman on the theater. Some of the luminaries in the audience were Cecil B. DeMille, Charlie Chaplin, and Jesse L. Lasky. Uncharacteristically, master showman Grauman did not make a speech, but then-mayor of Los Angeles, George Cryer, pretty much said it all when he took the podium. "I want to congratulate him [Grauman] upon his business sagacity in coming into this community...for the people of Los Angeles are proud of

Hollywood. We are proud of Hollywood and her beautiful homes; we are proud of her culture; and we are proud of her civic enterprise. May her future be filled with success— and success and all prosperity to Sid Grauman."

Grauman left the Egyptian in 1927 to reign at the new Chinese Theater just down the block. Following Grauman's departure, Fox West Coast Theaters leased the Egyptian as a re-run house through the Depression and the early years of World War II. In 1944, the theater was chosen by MGM as its exclusive Hollywood showcase and made a comeback to full glory.

In the late forties and fifties, the Egyptian, along with all the large movie palaces in the nation, underwent many renovations in an effort to lure the public away from their television sets and back to the theaters. Large screens and visual and sound gimmicks were popular additions. Modernization of the Egyptian included a new marquee, sign, box office, and a complete renovation of the charming courtyard entrance. The Egyptian got a new, massive curved Todd A-O screen in 1955 for the road show engagement of *Oklahoma*. To install the new screen, the entire stage was demolished, the pillars sphinxes and proscenium arch with Egyptian hieroglyphics were all removed. Wall-to-wall yellow drapes now covered almost the entire auditorium.

From 1955 to 1968, the Egyptian returned to its original roots as a theater that provided long-run reserved-seat road shows. *South Pacific* ran for more than a year, the colossal *Ben-Hur* opened in 1959 and sustained an incredible two-year engagement. *My Fair Lady* (1964) also ran for more than a year and finally *Funny Girl*, in 1968, was the last of the long-run road shows, and the last of the big star-studded premiere at the Egyptian.

United Artists was the last owner of the Egyptian Theater before it closed in 1992. The American Cinematheque purchased the theater from the city for $1 with the provision that this historical landmark would be restored to its original grandeur and re-opened as a movie theater showcasing the organizations celebrated, public programming.

Psychic Micahel J. Kouri has been to the Egyptian and claims that it is indeed haunted. Hopefully, we'll be able to go there soon and determine which ghostly moviegoers are enjoying the shows.

Exposition Park Rose Garden

A few minutes before sunset, partial apparitions of men and women dressed in 1920s and 30s clothing are frequently seen walking around the center fountain, while the transparent image of a girl dressed in white appears near roses on the west side.

The Gilmore Adobe

One of Southern California's oldest structures is the Gilmore Adobe built in 1852. It had two rooms with packed dirt floors and a brea roof from the La Brea Tar Pits. In 1880, Arthur Fremont Gilmore bought the house when he moved to LA from Illinois. He added a living room, wood floors, and a shingle roof. Over the years, he added plumbing and electricity. His son, Earl Bell Gilmore, was born there in 1887, and lived there until his death in 1964. In 1976, Earl's widow relocated

the AF Gilmore Company's corporate headquarters into the Adobe.

Arthur Gilmore was a successful dairy farmer drilling for water in 1901. Instead, he struck oil and formed the Gilmore Oil Company which became the largest oil company in the west. In 1936, Earl invented "Gas-a-terias"—the first self-serve gas stations. There is a replica of the original station across the street at the Farmer's Market. In another first, Arthur's son, Earl, was one of the first to use radio and jingles for promotion.

The land owned by the Gilmores eventually became the site of the world famous Farmer's Market, which was built in 1934, but before the market came to be, the first race car track designed for midget racers utilized the property, and after that came Gilmore Stadium, home to the first pro football team in LA. Gilmore Field was constructed in 1938 to accommodate the Hollywood Stars, a minor league professional baseball team of the Pacific Coast League, owned by Bing Crosby, Barbara Stanwyck, and Cecil B. DeMille.

Gilmore Field was perhaps the most intimate baseball venue ever created in a metropolitan area. Home plate was exactly thirty-four feet from the seats, first and third bases only twenty-four feet away. Gilmore Field taught a generation of Angelenos to love baseball. The Hollywood Stars popularity created the climate which helped persuade the owners of the Dodgers to move west, before the 1958 season.

Psychic Victoria Gross and I paid an unannounced visit to the old adobe a while back to see it for ourselves and in the hopes we could speak to someone in person about doing an investigation there.

Without knowing exactly where the old adobe sat, we walked all over The Grove and Farmer's Market trying to find it. Finally, we found someone who pointed us in the right direction and told us that the old adobe was actually across the street, hidden by tall hedges and set back from the street by a very long driveway.

When we got to the end of the driveway, the entrance was unlocked and we didn't see any *No Trespassing* signs so we casually strolled into the charming courtyard and had a quick look around. But almost immediately, dogs started barking, and it sounded like a huge pack about to be unleashed. Victoria and I looked at each other and quickly decided that we didn't want to become "dog food," so we spun around, took off like bats out of hell and ran out the way we came in.

A ghost hunter's quest is sometimes unsuccessful but it is never dull.

Blessed Sacrament Church

In the heart of old Hollywood, right next door to the famous Crossroads of the World on Sunset Boulevard, is an impressive structure, the Blessed Sacrament Church. Established back in 1904, it was the first Catholic church in the Hollywood area.

The groundbreaking finally took place on May 3, 1904, and building the church was truly a community event. All the work was done by volunteers from the parish and many of the raw building materials were either donated or paid for through individual contributions. To commemorate the church-raising, the names of the twenty-four families who made up the original congregation were put in a box

Blessed Sacrament Church as it looks today. A bit of old Hollywood still remains.

that was buried in the foundation cornerstone during a ceremony held on the 4th of July. This cornerstone is now situated in the patio between the church and the rectory. The finished church was modest in both size and appearance. The outside was painted a plain brown, and inside, the furnishings were spare. Although the small church only held 250 people, parishioners embraced it enthusiastically, as did the pastor who provided the church grounds with lush landscaping. Father Murphy planted palm trees and rose bushes and ivy, which soon covered the church's exterior walls. Almost immediately, Blessed Sacrament Church was considered a Hollywood landmark by the local residents, Catholic and non-Catholic alike.

The first Mass held in the new church took place on September 12, 1904, and was attended by fourteen adults and twenty-one children.

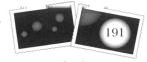

In 1923, in order to accommodate a growing population, the church broke ground at its present location.

During Tinsletown's heyday, this was the primary parish church for many of Hollywood's Catholic celebrities, including actresses Irene Dunne and Loretta Young.

This is the church where Bing Crosby got married to his first wife, Dixie Lee, back in September of 1930. Bing wasn't a rich man then, and the couple couldn't even afford to go on a honeymoon after the wedding.

In September of 1934, Russ Columbo, the fiancé of actress Carole Lombard, and a popular singer of stage, screen, and radio fame, accidentally shot himself while cleaning one of his guns. His funeral was held at the Church of the Blessed Sacrament; the pallbearers included Bing Crosby, Gilbert Roland, and Zeppo Marx. Columbo was buried at Forest Lawn Glendale.

As the Hollywood neighborhood around the church changed over the years, most of Blessed Sacrament's celebrity parishioners moved on to other parishes. That's not to say that the celebrity parishioners on the "otherside" have moved along with them.

The beautiful church remains with its integrity intact, and no doubt a handfull of faithful ghostly parishoners as well.

The Hollyhock House
4800 Hollywood Boulevard

Built between 1919 and 1921 for oil heiress Aline Barnsdall, Hollyhock House is Frank Lloyd Wright's first project in Los Angeles. Its namesake is abstracted and geometricized in much of the house's design, including exterior walls and interior furniture.

Hollyhock House was the centerpiece of a mostly unrealized Wright master plan for a theater community set on a thirty-six acre site, "Olive Hill." Wright left much of the supervision of construction of Hollyhock House to his son, landscape architect Lloyd Wright, and to architect Rudolf Schindler, as Wright himself was working on the Imperial Hotel in Tokyo (since destroyed).

In 1927, Aline Barnsdall donated the Hollyhock House and eleven surrounding acres to the City of Los Angeles for use as a public art park. It has been leased over the years to various arts organizations, necessitating a cycle of alteration and rehabilitation that is culminating in the large-scale rehabilitation which started in the fall of 1998. The rehabilitation is being partly funded by the lease of the property to the Los Angeles Mass Transit Authority for subway construction adjacent to the park. Today Hollyhock House is a part of Barnsdall Art Park, with a local art gallery, theater, and children's activities.

I spoke to someone who works in the house and she stated that one of the security guards claims that the building is haunted, but a formal investigation has not been approved at this juncture.

The Hollywood Bowl
2301 N. Highland Avenue

The world famous Hollywood Bowl is the largest natural amphitheater in the United States. Seating nearly 18,000 patrons, I'm really ashamed to admit this, but I've

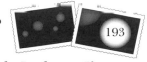
never actually been to the Hollywood Bowl. Perhaps I'm subconsciously harboring a grudge.

You see, I attended Hollywood High School, and back then, all of the Summer graduating classes traditionally had their graduation ceremony at the Hollywood Bowl. I really looked forward to it, but in my senior year, my school counselor decided that I had enough credits to skip a semester and I ended up graduating with the much smaller Winter class, whose graduation ceremony took place in the school auditorium.

The tradition of the graduation ceremonies began in June 1920 and has continued ever since, but some of us just missed out!

Built in 1919, the Bowl started it's life as a natural amphitheatre, formerly known as the Daisy Del. At first, the Bowl was very close to its natural state, with only makeshift wooden benches for the audience, and eventually a simple awning over the stage. In 1926, a group known as the Allied Architects was contracted to the Bowl, providing permanent seating and a shell. For the 1927 season, Lloyd Wright, son of famed architect Frank Lloyd Wright, built a pyramidal shell, with a vaguely Southwestern look, out of left-over lumber from a production of *Robin Hood*. This was generally regarded as the best shell the Bowl ever had from an acoustic standpoint; unfortunately, its appearance was deemed too avant-garde, and it was demolished at the end of the season. It did, however, get Wright a second chance, this time with the stipulation that the shell was to have an arch shape.

For the 1928 season, Wright built a fiberglass shell in the shape of concentric 120-degree arches, with movable panels inside that could be used to tune the acoustics. It was designed to be easily dismantled and stored between concert seasons; apparently for political reasons, this was not done, and it did not survive the winter.

Shortly thereafter, a permanant dome was erected and the bowl became host to the top names in the entertainment field.

Now home to the Los Angeles Philharmonic, it is the incomparable performances that have truly made the Hollywood Bowl's history unique. Legendary artists have appeared at the Bowl throughout the years: Sinatra, Pavarotti, Streisand, Stravinsky, and Heifetz have all graced the Hollywood Bowl stage, as have F.D.R., The Beatles, Mickey Rooney, Edward G. Robinson, Fonteyn and Nureyev, Nelson Eddy and Jeanette MacDonald, Simon and Garfunkel, and Abbott and Costello.

Baryshnikov has danced there, as has Fred Astaire. Garth Brooks, Nat "King" Cole, Ella Fitzgerald, Billie Holiday, Elton John, Al Jolson, and Judy Garland have headlined star-studded shows at the Bowl, but the all-time attendance record of 26,410 paid admissions was set on August 7, 1936, for a performance by the diminutive French opera star, Lily Pons.

The Hollywood Bowl has served movie society across the decades as the place to be seen. Among the listed box holders for the 1928 season were: C. Chaplin (#117), Mr. and Mrs. Cecil B. De Mille (#641), William De Mille (#736), Sid Grauman (#136), Alexander Korda (#113), Robert Z. Leonard (#143), Adolphe Menjou (#528), Conrad Nagel (#734), and Fay Wray (#861).

Do the ghosts of past performers still haunt the Hollywood Bowl stage, and do the spirits of appreciative audiences relive their favorite performances of long ago? I think so.

The Whisky. An icon of the famous Sunset Strip.

The Whisky

An anchor on the Sunset Strip since it's opening in 1964, the Whisky A Go-Go has played host to rock 'n' roll's most important bands, from the Doors, Janis Joplin, and Led Zeppelin to today's up-and-coming new artists. They say the rock and roll scene in Los Angeles was born when the Whisky started operation. The Whisky played an important role in many musical careers, especially for bands based in Southern California. The Byrds, Alice Cooper, Buffalo Springfield, and Love were regulars, and The Doors were the house band for a while.

Van Morrison's band, Them, had a two-week residency in June, 1966, with The Doors as the opening act. On the last night, they all jammed together on "Gloria." Frank Zappa's

Mothers of Invention got their record contract based on a performance at the Whisky. Jimi Hendrix came by to jam when Sam and Dave headlined. Otis Redding recorded his album, "In Person," at the Whiskey a Go Go in 1966. The Turtles performed there when their newest (and biggest-selling) single "Happy Together" was becoming a hit, only to lose their new bassist, Chip Douglas (who had arranged the song), to the Monkees; guitarist Michael Nesmith invited him to become their producer. (He returned to the Turtles a year later, to produce them.) Neil Diamond also played at the Whisky on occasion. Chicago Transit Authority (later Chicago) was also a house band until discovered by Jimi Hendrix and brought on tour in 1968. Many British performers made their first headlining performances in the area at the Whisky, including The Kinks, The Who, Cream, Led Zeppelin, Roxy Music, and Oasis.

The Whisky fell on hard times once the first flush of punk rock lost steam, and closed its doors in 1982. It reopened in 1986 as a "four-wall," a venue that could be rented by promoters and bands. Although a few booths remain on the perimeter, the interior has mostly been transformed into a bare, seatless space where the audience is forced to stand throughout the performances. A few sets of tables and chairs remain in the upstairs area, but these are often roped off as a "VIP" section, reserved for special guests of the bands, record executives, etc.

The Whisky A Go-Go became the principal hangout of musicians and hipsters in Hollywood in the 1960s. The Beach Boys played there in 1971.

Clubs like the Whisky are high energy venues and the perfect atmosphere to attract spirits, so I can't image the landmark being a ghost-free zone. This is another place that I hope will be open to having an investigation one day soon.

House of Blues
8430 Sunset Boulevard

The House of Blues is a chain of music halls and restaurants founded in 1992 by Hard Rock Cafe founder Isaac Tigrett and his friend and investor Dan Aykroyd. It is a home for live music and southern-inspired cuisine, whose clubs celebrate African-American culture, specifically blues music and folk art.

The West Hollywood branch opened in April of 1994 by none other than Elwood Blues himself: actor Dan Aykroyd.

Located in the heart of the Sunset Strip on the spot where the old John Barrymore's estate used to

The House of Blues by day. But who haunts it by night?

be, the exterior of the House of Blues resembles a giant tin shack. It was inspired by an old, metal cotton gin at the famous "crossroads" outside of Clarksdale, Mississippi, where Highways 61 and 49 meet, and where (according to legend) the father of the delta blues, Robert Johnson, sold his soul to the Devil in return for his musical talent.

The owners imported the corrugated tin from that Southern gin mill, and even put genuine Mississippi mud under the stage and in the planters.

The House of Blues quickly became a hot spot for Hollywood celebrities including Bruce Springsteen, Brad Pitt, Madonna, Kevin Costner, Woody Harrelson, Sly Stallone, Goldie Hawn, Sally Field, Wesley Snipes, Sandra Bullock, Heather Locklear, Leonard Nimoy, Matthew Modine, Smokey Robinson, John Bon Jovi, and the one and only James Brown. O.J. Simpson and his wife, Nicole, were seen here with Byron Allen just a few weeks before the infamous murders.

In 2003, the club was unfortunately involved in a celebrity scandal. Famed record producer Phil Spector met actress Lana Clarkson at the House of Blues, where she was working as a hostess. They went back to his mansion in Alhambra, but after dropping them off, the chauffeur heard gunshots. The police were called, Clarkson's body was found in the marble foyer of the thirty-three-room home, and Spector was arrested for murder.

Given the club's history, I called the House of Blues to find out whether it would be possible to schedule and investigation and was told several stories about ghostly happenings. The person I spoke to was certain that she was working in a haunted house. Exact dates for checking

out this super spooky spot have not been nailed down just yet...but stay tuned... Who do you think is haunting the House of Blues? My money is on ... well let's wait and see...

Hollywood Athletic Club

This big white landmark, built in 1924, once housed a private residential club which was founded by Cecil B. DeMille and was at one time very popular with actors. Charlie Chaplin was an early habitué. A huge gym that used to be on the premises attracted macho types: Cornel Wilde was a lifeguard at the pool where Weissmuller and Buster Crabbe swam laps and into which, it is said, Errol Flynn took whizzes from two stories above. Stood up by Flynn, Jean Harlow arrived here once wearing only a coat. And on another legendary night, John Barrymore was brought here by friends for a final drink—Barrymore was freshly dead at the time. Departing from his image as an upstanding American, John Wayne was known to stand on the roof, throwing billiard balls at passing vehicles. In 1949, the first Emmy Awards were held here -- a bronze plaque recalls the event. The pool has been converted to a ballroom; now the place is a dance hall and restaurant whose patrons include a sampling of the local talent.

Many sources claim that the location is quite haunted and I tend to agree. Hopefully, an opportunity to find out for myself will soon be forthcoming.

C.C. Browns Hollywood Boulevard and Orange Drive

C.C. Brown's 2008.

C.C. Browns began in 1906 as a family-owned ice cream shop. It remained a family-operated business until closing on June 8th, 1996. Candy maker Clarence Clifton Brown brought his copper kettles out to Los Angeles by covered wagon and opened his ice cream shop ninety years ago. The shop has been revered by chocolate lovers as the birthplace of the hot fudge sundae. In 1924, he passed the shop on to his son, Cliff, and the store moved from downtown Los Angeles to Hollywood where it became popular with celebrities. In 1963, Cliff sold

the store to his friend, John Schumacher, a Carnation Dairy chemist.

In its heyday, the ice cream shop was the favorite hangout of the Hollywood elite, who would often stop in after watching their films at Graumann's Chinese Theater just a block away. It's been said that fans didn't pester the actors because the real star at Brown's was their hot fudge sundae.

A regular spot for Hollywood hopefuls, it's been written that both Judy Garland and Bob Hope used to work there, and during the halcyon days of the big premier, the most celebrated names in the entertainment industry frequented the sweet shop. Fans used to line up outside Brown's for hours while great stars like Joan Crawford and Marlon Brando signed autographs.

Actress Ellen Drew was discovered at Brown's. While working at the ice cream parlor, customer William Demarest took notice of her and was instrumental in having her put under contract at Paramount Studios in 1936.

C.C. Brown's always made its classic sundae with French vanilla ice cream, chopped roasted almonds, and real home-made whipping cream, served it in a silver goblet with the Hot Fudge Sauce in a small brown pitcher on the side. Brown's closed its doors in 1996, and the building now houses one of Hollywood's many souvenir shops, but one can't help but hope that perhaps after closing, the smell of hot fudge is in the air accompanied by the laughter of the celebrities that used to dine there.

Famous Last Words

Bugsy Siegel's plaque at Hollywood memorial Cemetery.

I've always been fascinated with epitaphs, especially those that make me smile, like, "Here lies the body of Margaret Bent. She kicked up her heels and away she went." Or, "Here lies Butch, we planted him raw. He was quick on the trigger but slow on the draw." And then there was the one-liner left behind by my friend, writer Stanley Ralph Ross, "Thanks, I had a wonderful time."

I think we all have some clever line that we'd like to see written on our tombstones, reminding those we leave behind of who we are or what final message we'd like to impart. Here is a list of true celebrity epitaphs. Some you will find amusing, others include a trademark phrase, a

reminder of who they were or a fond remembrance left behind by a loved one. Whether ghost, ghostly, or just creative, Hollywood lives on...

Epitaphs

Merv Griffin: "I will not be right back after this message"

Dean Martin: "Everybody Loves Somebody Sometime"

Mel Blanc: "That's All Folks!"

Minnie Ripperton: "Loving You is Easy Cause You're Beautiful"

Frank Sinatra: "The Best Is yet To Come"

Karen Carpenter: "A star on earth—a star in heaven"

Sammy Davis, Jr.: "The Entertainer, He Did It All"

George Burns and Gracie Allen: "Together Again"

Ernie Kovacs: "Nothing in Moderation. We all loved him"

John Barrymore: "Goodnight Sweet Prince"

Rita Hayworth: "To Yesterday's Companionship
and Tomorrow's Reunion"

John Belushi: "I May Be Gone,
But Rock and Roll Lives On"

Sonny Bono: "And The Beat Goes On"

Joe Derita: "The Last Stooge"

Andy Gibb: "An Everlasting Love"

Joan Hackett: "Go Away—I'm Asleep"

George Reeves: "Superman"

Lawrence Welk: "Keep A Smile In Your Heart"

Jackie Gleason: "And Away We Go"

Jack Lemmon: "Jack Lemmon
In"

Billy Barty: "In Loving Memory of Billy Barty
Who Always Thought Big"

Francis Bavier: "Aunt Bee"

Irene Ryan: "Granny"

Rodney Dangerfield: "There Goes the Neighborhood"

Bette Davis: "She Did It The Hard Way"

Cass Elliott: Adorned with musical notes

Sam Kinison: "In another time and place
he would have been called a prophet."

LaWanda Page: "Aunt Esther"

Phil Silvers: "Comedian"

Lorne Greene: "The World's Best Loved Father
—Ben Cartwright"

Jack Benny: "A Gentle Man"

Ted Knight: "Bye, Guy"

Wallace Berry: "No man is indispensable,
but some are irreplaceable."

Jack Oakie: "In a simple double-take,
thou hast more than voice e'er spake;
When you hear laughter,
that wonderful sound,
you know that Jack Oakie's around"

Clara Bow: "Hollywood's 'It' Girl"

Casey Stengle: "There comes a time in every man's life
and I've had plenty

Elmo Lincoln: "The First Tarzan"

Benjamin "Bugsy" Siegel: "In loving memory
from the family"

Richard Conte: "A man of many talents and graces,
loved by a thousand unknown faces.
1910-1975--?"

Michael Landon: "He seized life with joy.
He gave generously.
He leaves a legacy of love and
laughter."

Dinah Shore: "Loved by all who knew her
and millions who never did"

Animator Isadore "Friz" Freleng:
"He shared his talent with the World"

Alongside the inscription are several of Warner Brothers best-known cartoon characters including Bugs Bunny, Porky Pig, Daffy Duck, Tweety Bird, and Elmer Fudd, all wearing tuxedoes and standing in a high-kicking chorus line.

Norman Fell: "A greatly talented and romantic
man."

Lee J. Cobb: "Ay, every inch a king."

John Barrymore: "Alas, Poor Yorick"

It's also fascinating to hear what some people say on their deathbeds, so here are a few famous last words.

"Codeine . . . bourbon."
—Tallulah Bankhead

"Is everybody happy?
I want everybody to be happy.
I know I'm happy"
—Ethel Barrymore

"Die? I should say not, dear fellow.
No Barrymore would allow such
a conventional thing to happen to him."
—John Barrymore

"I should never have switched from Scotch to Martinis."
—Humphrey Bogart

"That was the best ice-cream soda I ever tasted."
—Lou Costello

"Damn it . . . Don't you dare ask God to help me."
—Joan Crawford,
to her housekeeper, who had begun to pray aloud

"That was a great game of golf, fellers."
—Harry Lillis "Bing" Crosby

"I've never felt better."
—Douglas Fairbanks, Sr.

When the priest, who was attending him on his deathbed, said, "May the Lord have mercy on your soul," **Charlie Chaplin** quickly replied, "Why not? After all, it belongs to him."

"God damn the whole f----' world
and everyone in it but you, Carlotta."
—W.C. Fields

"This is it! I'm going. I'm going."
—Al Jolson

"I'm tired. I'm going back to bed."
—George Reeves

"I've had a hell of a lot of fun
and I've enjoyed every minute of it."
—Errol Flynn

"Yes, it's tough, but not as tough as doing comedy."
—Edmond Gwynn,
when asked if he thought dying was tough

"Nothing matters. Nothing matters."
—Louis B. Mayer

"I knew it. I knew it. Born in a hotel room
—and God damn it—died in a hotel room."
—Eugene O'Neill

"Don't worry chief, it will be alright."
—Rudolph Valentino

"Dear World, I am leaving you because I am bored
I feel I have lived long enough.
I am leaving you with your worries
in this sweet cesspool—good luck. "
—Suicide note written by **George Sanders**

Contributors

David Wells

David Wells says he had a very ordinary family upbringing in a small Scottish village. His mother worked in a knitwear factory and his father was a coal miner. At the age of sixteen he joined The Royal Navy, left when he was twenty-four and began a career in catering within hotels and leisure clubs. In 1991, David decided to go back to college to study leisure as a career and to fund this he was working forty hours a week as a chef and a waiter in a small hotel in the south of England.

While on Christmas Holiday in Scotland in 1992, David wound up in the hospital, severely ill with pneumonia. As he tells it, "On the second night in hospital, I found myself in the corridor being told to go back to bed by an old lady. She said that this is not my time and I have work to do. I did as she asked only to find I was already there! Thinking nothing more than I had been dreaming, I forgot the incident and was released a few days later when improvements to my health were great enough. I returned to England and was convalescing when I started to experience odd happenings in my home, so odd that I found it impossible to sleep and was looking not so fresh. A friend suggested that I visited a woman who 'knew about these things' and I duly did."

He then went on to learn astrology to ground his abilities, which were showing themselves at an alarming rate. His memory of talking to relatives that had passed over when he was a child came back and he realized that being a psychic medium was his true vocation.

David is the author of *David Wells' Complete Guide To Developing Your Psychic Skills* and *Past, Present and Future: What Your Past Lives Tell You About Yourself*, and has just completed his third book, also dealing with the subject of past lives. He recently left *Most Haunted* and is now devoting his time to writing books, conducting workshops, and giving lectures both in the UK and here in the United States.

Victoria Gross

Paranormal researcher and investigator Victoria Gross has been doing professional psychic readings since 1987. Her background is in Tarot, Palmistry, Crystal Gazing, and Psychometry. She also teaches, lectures, and does workshops on these and various subjects relating to metaphysics. Victoria trained at The Arthur Findlay College in England for mediumship, is the founder of The North Orange County Tarot Society located in Southern California, and a member of The International Paranormal Research Organization.

She has just completed her first book, *The Ghosts of Orange County* and is working on another book as well.

Barry Conrad

Barry Conrad originally hails from Hamilton, Ohio. When Conrad was twelve years old, he overheard a friend of his mother's discussing the paranormal incidents taking place in her new home on the outskirts of Fairfield, Ohio. Doors would slam shut of their own accord, objects moved around, and the all-pervasive odor of smoke would sometimes filter through the house. One night, her son nearly jumped from the balcony of an upstairs bedroom, feeling that he was being asphyxiated by an invisible fire. Barry was impressed by the woman's apparent sincerity and that lead to his interest in supernatural matters.

He worked as a TV news cameraman at WKRC-TV in Cincinnati working under the auspices of anchorman/reporter Nick Clooney (father of actor George Clooney), and in 1986, Barry moved to California to start his own production company called American Video Features (now known as Barcon Video).

During the fall of 1987, Conrad met Dr. Barry Taff who had once investigated a woman's claims that she had been raped and attacked by an invisible force.

The story became a motion picture in 1983 called *The Entity*. Thereafter, Taff and Conrad developed a working relationship that lasts to this day, as they have investigated dozens of haunted houses and poltergeist cases in the Los Angeles area. In 1989, one of those cases turned out to be nearly as frightening as *The Entity*. While checking into a woman's story in San Pedro of malevolent ghostly activity, including the sighting of a disembodied head, the pair encountered violent phenomena. Conrad filmed the case and later made it into a documentary titled *An Unknown Encounter*. Segments of the story later appeared in an anthology film that he produced in 2002 called *California's Most Haunted*. Both shows garnered high ratings when they aired on the Sci-Fi Channel's *Tuesday De-classified* series in 2003.

Scott Michaels

Hollywood historian and owner of Dearly Departed Tours, Scott Michaels, is well known in Hollywood as a Master of the Macabre. He's a walking encyclopedia of where the rich and famous died and how they met their makers.

"I've been interested in death since I was a tyke," says Scott, "My mother recalls taking me to a funeral of a young family member when I was three years old. On the way to the grave site, I noticed the tent set up, and asked, 'Mom, are we going to the circus?' I suppose in a way, we were."

In addition to Dearly Departed, Scott also has his own website, the infamous findadeath.com.

Scott's credibility as an expert on Hollywood deaths is unparalleled and he's been featured in dozens of televisions shows, newspaper, and magazine articles, and is a regular on Liza Gibbons' radio show.

Kenny Kingston

L egendary celebrity psychic Kenny Kingston was born to the seventh daughter of a seventh daughter - a very psychic sign.

He credits three women in his life with helping him to develop his psychic ability: his grandmother, Catherine Walsh Clark, taught him to read tea leaves when he was 4 years old; his beloved mother Kaye taught him psychometry (touching an object and picking up psychic vibrations from it) when he was seven; and legendary film immortal (and family friend) Mae West taught him clairaudio (listening to a voice and picking up psychic vibrations) when he was nine years old.

Throughout his childhood and as a young adult, Kenny gave psychic messages and readings to friends and neighbors, many of whom were involved in politics and show business. Word spread and soon he was performing on radio and television, as well as appearing live in lectures.

Kenny has appeared on more television shows than any other psychic, guesting repeatedly on major talk shows around the world. He has hosted his own television series

twice - *Kenny Kingston: A Psychic Experience* in the late 1970's in the Los Angeles area; and the syndicated *Kenny Kingston Show* on the East coast during the 1990's.

Kenny has given readings and messages to Marilyn Monroe (he was her one and only psychic), Lucille Ball, Greta Garbo, U.S. Presidents Eisenhower and Truman, Whoopi Goldberg, Phyllis Diller, Howie Mandel, Cindy Williams and many others. His ties to British royalty began with the Duke and Duchess of Windsor and continued to other members of the monarchy. He has written five books on the psychic world, including his best selling book, *I Still Talk To.*

Kenny lives by the motto: "Only Believe, All Things are Possible if You Only Believe."

Mark Nelson

Psychic medium Mark Nelson had his first paranormal experience as an 11-year-old boy. A few days after his father's funeral, Mark saw his father standing at the edge of his property.

Today, Mark works as a psychic medium in the Los Angeles area. One of his unique gifts is that of psychometry. By simply holding personal effects such as a watch, keys, a ring

or pair of glasses, Mark is able to connect with spirits, and provide valuable guidance for the living. Mark has used his highly accurate abilities in paranormal investigations from college dorms in Maine to murder scenes in Los Angeles. He currently has clients who call him for readings from a Hawaii to New England. Mark is also the host of Positively Psychic on Para-X radio, where he's interviewed some of the best-known psychic mediums of our time, including Allison Dubois, John Holland, Chris Fleming, and Derek Acorah. He's also appeared on the E-Channel, won the title of "Most Gifted," on a pilot for FOX Television, is a proud father and husband, and loves looking for ghosts with Marla Brooks. You can learn more about Mark, watch some of his TV appearances, request a reading, and more at his official site, www.positivelypsychic.com.

Michael J. Kouri

Michael J. Kouri has known of his psychic abilities since childhood and is currently the published author of twenty-six books related to the subjects of parapsychology, Psychic Phenomena, and Antiques, as he is also an Antique Appraiser who conducts Estate Sales throughout the state of California—many of which have been haunted. He is the creator/producer and host of his own television show: *Investigating the Unknown with Michael J. Kouri* and has appeared on dozens of international television shows with *Barbara Walters* on *The View, 20/20, T.V. Guide Channel's Pre–Emmy Show with Joan Rivers, KOCE's Real Orange with Rick Milkie*, Warner Bros. production of *Ghost Ships—Queen Mary in Long Beach, California*, French Television's *Ghost Hunters of the World*, BBC's *Dead Famous on A&E & the Discovery Channel*, The History Channel's *Haunted Alcatraz*, The Travel Channel's *America's Most Haunted Places, True Hauntings & Ghost Stories of Southern California*, ABC Television's *America's Scariest Ghosts Caught on Videotape, Unsolved Mysteries, Mystic Journey's–Haunted Hollywood*, FOX Family Channel's *Exploring the Unknown*, to name a few...

Barry Shainbaum

Barry Shainbaum is an icon of survival and success. Today he is a renowned public speaker, broadcaster, and celebrated photographer, acclaimed for documenting some of the world's most famous and heroic individuals. He has been featured in the *Los Angeles Times*, FOX TV - New York City, *Toronto Star*, *Toronto Sun*, Canada AM, Breakfast TV, TV Ontario, Court TV, and numerous radio stations across North America.

Glossary

An **Anomaly**, in paranormal terms, refers to any phenomena that we cannot explain.

An **Apparition** refers to any ghost that seems to have material substance. If it appears in any physical form, including a vapor-like image, it may be called an apparition. It can also be explained as the visual appearance of a person whose physical body is not present.

Clearing, or space clearing is the process of ridding an area of lingering unpleasant energy. Space clearing may encourage ghosts to cross over, or at least to leave the haunted location. At times, though, attempting to clear a space of an unwanted spirit may result in even stronger activity than before for an extended period of time.

Demon or Evil Entities seem to be spirits that are either evil in nature, or are actually demons. Demons are commonly considered to be things that have not lived as humans, and seem to take delight in terrorizing humans. Some think demons may even be able to interfere with and affect human kind.

Earthbound Spirits are people who have passed over but do not realize their true condition or choose to stick around and impose themselves on the living. The result is hauntings and occasionally possessions.

Ectoplasm is the physical residue of psychic energy. Ectoplasm can be seen by the naked eye, and is best viewed in dark settings since it is translucent and tends to glow.

EVP (Electronic Voice Phenomena) is the recording of unexplained voices, usually in haunted settings. Many times, no

sound is heard while the recording is being made. It's only upon playback that the voices can be heard.

An **Entity** is something that has a distinct, separate existence from our own.

A **Ghost** is a sentient entity or spirit that visits or lingers in our world, after he or she lived among us as a human being. There is also evidence of ghostly animals. It is a form of apparition, usually the visual appearance of a deceased human's spirit or soul.

Haunting describes a setting where ghosts, poltergeists, and/ or residual energy seem to produce significant paranormal activity. Recurrent sounds of human activity, sightings of apparitions, and other psychic phenomena, in a location when no one is there physically are all signs of a haunting.

Intelligent Hauntings may be by a ghost or a demon. With an intelligent haunting, the entity is aware of its surroundings, including living people who may be present. This entity may be either benevolent, malevolent, or benign.

Malevolent Hauntings are done by a ghost or demon that seeks to inflict harm on the living.

Manifestation is the materialized form of a spirit.

A **Medium** is a person who possesses the ability to communicate with spirits of the deceased. Some mediums claim to be able to channel the spirit, by allowing the deceased to speak or write messages using the medium's body.

Orbs are round, whitish or pastel colored translucent areas that appear as balls of light and may occasionally seem to be moving. While there has been no substantial proof that the balls of light are

associated with ghosts, the dead or any paranormal behavior, many believe that orbs are the human soul or life force of those that once inhabited a physical body here on earth.

The Other Side is a term used to describe the spirit world, or the place spirits go after death beyond our physical plane.

In the word **Paranormal**, the prefix, "para" indicates something that is irregular, faulty, or operating outside the usual boundaries. Paranormal is an umbrella term used to describe a wide variety of reported anomalous phenomena. According to the Journal of Parapsychology, the term paranormal describes "any phenomenon that in one or more respects exceeds the limits of what is deemed physically possible according to current scientific assumptions."

Phenomenon is an unusual, profound, or unexplainable fact or occurrence.

Place memory is information about past events that is stored in the physical environment.

The word **Poltergeist** comes from the German word meaning "noisy ghost." This term has been in use since the early nineteenth century to mean a spirit that makes noise, or otherwise plays pranks and is often annoying. Poltergeists can move from one location to another, following the person they've chosen to torment.

A **Portal** literally means a doorway or gate, and in paranormal terms, it suggests a specific location through which spirits enter and leave our world. When there are multiple phenomena in a confined area, such as an abundance of unexplained orbs, some people call this a ghost portal.

Psychic is a word used to describe an occurrence, ability, or event that is sensed without the use of the five known human senses of

sight, hearing, taste, touch, and smell. People who are said to possess psychic abilities are referred to as "psychics."

With **Residual Energy**, many believe that emotionally charged events leave an imprint or energy residue on the physical objects nearby.

Residual Haunting is a term used to describe a ghost that is trapped in a continuous loop. Another theory is that an event left a psychic impression on an area and some people are able to witness a replay of that scene. What distinguishes residual energy from an active haunting is that the energy/impressions repeat consistently, as if on a loop. The energy levels may increase or decrease, but the content remains the same with each manifestation. By contrast, in what we term an active haunting, the ghost may respond to environmental stimuli and direct contact.

Spirit is a word that comes from the Latin, meaning "that which animates life," or "the soul of the being." In paranormal terms, spirits are electromagnetic entities in the forms of orbs, mists, vortexes, or shadows, which are the signature of a once-living person who has returned to a specific location. Their nature is interactive as opposed to residual.

Spirit photography captures the image of a ghost on film. Many of these are supposedly intended as a mere portrait of a living human being, but when the film is developed, an ethereal ghostly face or figure can be seen hovering near the subject. This may also incorporate orbs, vortexes, and mists to some degree.

Supernatural relates to an occurrence in violation of the laws of nature. Spiritualism contends that the phenomena of the séance room are ruled by as yet unknown laws and rejects the term.